JUDICIAL EXCERPTS
GOVERNING
STUDENTS AND TEACHERS

By

Edward C. Bolmeier

Professor Emeritus of Education

Duke University

THE MICHIE COMPANY

Law Publishers

CHARLOTTESVILLE, VIRGINIA

This book is dedicated to my beloved grandchildren,

JACK, SUSAN, ANN, AND SARAH

CONTENTS

v

INTRODUCTION

While teaching school law for several decades and reviewing the school cases reported weekly in the regional and federal reporters systems, certain judicial passages have left lasting impressions. It seems to this author that selected excerpts from these passages which are most significant because of their precedence, eloquence and logical reasoning are worthy of reproduction.

Limited scope of the undertaking. In view of the fact that hundreds of school law cases are reported yearly, it is obviously necessary to select the judicial excerpts which are the most notable and interesting to the student of school law, or to anyone else concerned with the legal principles gleaned from court opinions which guide educators in the progress of the schools.

Admittedly, selection of judicial excerpts by this writer may not be in harmony with that of others who are especially interested in the many other areas of school law. For example, despite the importance of litigation concerning such matters as school finance and school property, the main emphasis here will be focused on cases involving the student and the teacher. Judicial comments concerning the "human rights" of students and teachers will be particularly stressed.

Although this study is restricted to legal issues involving students and teachers, there is no restriction with respect to the era in which judicial opinions have been rendered. In fact, some of the earliest declarations of judges and justices stand out as "judicial gems" even though they may no longer be in tune with later day social and political conditions. The merits of a judicial

1

declaration should be judged on the basis of social and political attitudes that prevail at the time the declaration is made.

Recognition of dissenting opinions. Even though the majority opinions of the court determine the ruling decision of a case, many dissenting opinions are worthy of review. To many people the dissenting opinions of such renowned justices as Frankfurter, Black, Stone and Douglas make as much sense as the majority opinions. For example, the weight of a dissenting opinion written by Justice Stone concerning the flag salute case (*Gobitis*) turned out to be the essence of the majority opinion in a later flag salute case (*Barnette*).

Justice Stewart is not known as "the great dissenter." Nevertheless, he is remembered as "the lone dissenter" in the Bible reading and prayer cases. His views as expressed in his dissents stand out as being logical and are strongly supported by many citizens today.

In the chapters which follow, excerpts will be quoted from dissenting opinions as well as the majority opinions — especially from cases decided by the United States Supreme Court.

The great majority of school cases reaching the United States Supreme Court are related to the "human rights" provisions of the Constitution, spelled out most specifically in the amendments. The First Amendment and the Fourteenth Amendment have especially been involved in cases dealing with due process of law, racial discrimination and religious influences in the public schools. Less frequently, the Fifth Amendment, dealing with self-incrimination, has been referred to in cases involving alleged subversive affiliation. Also the Eighth

Amendment, which refers to "cruel, and unusual punishments" has come into focus in cases involving student disciplinary practices — especially corporal punishment.

Organization and treatment of cases. Rather than merely referring to cases in a chronological and unrelated manner, the author attempts to categorize the cases in a logical order with the intent that the publication may serve as a textbook for students in school law classes as well as a reference book for school personnel and officials.

Part I deals with cases involving the *student.* Attention is given to such matters as (1) compulsory and prohibitory school attendance, (2) authority over curricular and extracurricular activities, (3) regulatory control over the student and (4) student disciplinary practices.

Part II deals with cases involving the *teacher.* Attention is given to such matters as (1) right of association, (2) grounds for teacher dismissal, (3) teachers' rights outside the classroom, (4) right to strike, (5) liability for pupil injury and (6) sexuality and the teacher.

Subjective treatment in the publication will be held to a minimum. Of course, the issue involved in a case must be stated as well as the decision rendered by the court. Mainly, however, excerpts from the majority and minority opinions of the courts will be cited as they are published in official law reporters.

In selecting the cases to be treated (with certain modifications) in this publication, the author has referred to some of the memorable and significant cases discussed in his most recent publications — particularly

(1) *"Legal Limits of Authority over the Pupil,"* The Michie Company, 1970; (2) *"Teachers' Legal Rights, Restraints and Liabilities,"* The W. H. Anderson Company, 1971; (3) *"The School in the Legal Structure,"* 2nd edition, The W. H. Anderson Company, 1973; (4) *"Landmark Supreme Court Decisions on Public School Issues,"* The Michie Company, 1973; (5) *"Sex Litigation and the Public Schools,"* The Michie Company, 1975; and (6) *"Legality of Student Disciplinary Practices,"* The Michie Company, 1976.

Part I

COURT CASES INVOLVING THE STUDENT

PRELUDE

As a *prelude* to the chapters which are included in Part I (Court Cases Involving the Student), the following introductory passage is quoted from this author's text, *"Legal Limits of Authority over the Pupil":*

Allocation of authority over the pupil has been a matter of dispute and litigation ever since the beginning of public education in America. The courts have been called upon repeatedly to settle issues concerning "parental versus state authority over the Pupil."

The judicial task of delimiting family and school authority over the pupil is a difficult one. The pupil, as a subject of the state, is entitled to the rights and freedoms thereof, and at the same time he is subject to those regulations of the state which are designed for the health, safety, progress and general welfare of the populace. But the pupil is also a member of the family, and in this capacity, is subject to the care and control of parents.

When clashes between the family and the school arise over matters concerning the pupil's welfare, the courts must take into consideration the natural rights as well as the civil rights of pupils and their parents. *Natural rights* are considered to be "inalienable,"

5

"fundamental" and "inherent"; they are rights necessary to personal liberty, security and the pursuit of happiness. *Civil rights,* on the other hand, are those rights which pertain to an individual by virtue of his citizenship as a resident in a community or state. Whereas natural rights are considered to exist outside of law and independent of government, civil rights exist under law guaranteed by federal and state constitutions. Civil rights include personal freedoms such as religious liberty, freedom of speech, security against unreasonable search and seizure, the guaranty against self-incrimination, the right to trial by jury and the right to equal protection of the laws. Both natural rights and civil rights, such as those enumerated, are frequently brought into focus when pupils and their parents challenge, in the courts, unfavorable actions of school officials. Then on the basis of humanity and law the courts make the final decisions.

Chapter 1

COMPULSORY AND PROHIBITORY
SCHOOL ATTENDANCE

§ 1.1 Evolving state versus parental authority.

The state's authority over the pupil is expressed in state constitutions and in the statutes. Many of the statutes are vague and brief regarding who and under what conditions a child may be compelled to or prohibited from attending a public school. Consequently, much controversy and litigation have evolved, necessitating the judiciary to serve as the arbiter of disputes between the school and the parents of a child whose attendance falls within the legal compulsory school attendance limits. Several judicial opinions on the issue follow:

1. *Rulison v. Post*, 79 Ill. 567, 28 N.E. 68 (1876).

In this earliest reported case, the court upheld parental authority as indicated by the excerpt from its opinion:

> Even if, under our constitution, the General Assembly has the power to provide for compulsory education, they have adopted no law looking to such a system; nor can we suppose that any body of practical men, in

7

adopting such a system, would ever endeavor to compel generally what is known as liberal education.

Parents and guardians are under the responsibility of preparing children intrusted to their care and nurture, for the discharge of their duties in life. Law-givers in all free countries and, with few exceptions, in despotic governments, have deemed it wise to leave the education and nurture of the children of the State to the direction of the parent or guardian. This is, and has ever been, the spirit of our free institutions. The State has provided the means and brought them within the reach of all to acquire the benefits of a common school education, but leaves it to the parents and guardians to determine the extent to which they will render it available to the children under their charge (*Id.* at 573).

2. *Board of Education v. Purse,* 101 Ga. 422, 28 S.E. 896 (1897).

Even though parental authority was permitted by common law practice, the courts soon began to be critical of the practice, as indicated by the following paragraph of the court's opinion:

While the common law recognizes this as a duty of great importance, there was no remedy provided for the child in case this duty was not discharged by the parent. The child, at the will of the parent, could be allowed to grow up in ignorance, and become a more than useless

8

member of society, and for this great wrong, brought about by the neglect of his parents, the common law provided no remedy. Not only no remedy was given to the child, but no punishment was inflicted upon the parent (*Id.* at 899).

3. *State v. Bailey,* 157 Ind. 324, 61 N.E. 730 (1901).

Finally, in 1901, the Indiana judiciary broke with the common law practice by declaring the state's authority to compel school attendance of children regardless of the parent's wishes. An excerpt of the court's opinion follows:

The natural rights of a parent to the custody and control of his infant child are subordinate to the power of the state, and may be restricted and regulated by municipal laws. One of the most important natural duties of the parent is his obligation to educate his child, and this duty he owes not to the child only, but to the commonwealth. If he neglects to perform it or willingly refuses to do so, he may be coerced by law to execute such civil obligations. The welfare of the child and the best interests of society require that the state shall exert its sovereign authority to secure to the child the opportunity to acquire an education. Statutes making it compulsory upon the parent, guardian, or other person having the custody and control of children to send them to public or private schools for longer or shorter periods during certain years of the life of such children have not only been upheld as strictly within the constitutional power of the legislature, but have generally been regarded necessary to carry out the express purposes of the constitution itself (*Id.* at 731-32).

§ 1.2 Alternatives to public school attendance.

After the main issue of compulsory school attendance has been resolved, the courts are faced with the question as to whether the compulsory attendance requirement can be met by attending a *nonpublic* school.

1. *Pierce v. Society of Sisters of Holy Names,* 268 U.S. 510, 45 S. Ct. 571 (1925).

The issue in this precedential case was whether a child might satisfy the compulsory school attendance law by attending a *private* school.

The United States Supreme Court declared unconstitutional an Oregon statute which required attendance at a *public* school only. A brief excerpt from the court's classic opinion, which has been generally unchallenged, follows:

> . . . we think it entirely plain that the Act of 1922 unreasonably interferes with the liberty of parents and guardians to direct the upbringing and education of children under their control. . . . The fundamental theory of liberty upon which all governments in this Union repose excludes any general power of the state to standardize its children by forcing them to accept instruction from public teachers

only. The child is not the mere creature of the state; those who nurture him and direct his destiny have a right, coupled with the high duty, to recognize and prepare him for additional obligations (45 S. Ct. 571, at 573).

2. *Rice v. Commonwealth,* 188 Va. 224, 49 S.E.2d 342 (1948).

Despite the fact that attendance at a *qualified private* school may satisfy the compulsory school attendance law, that concession is not made by home instruction where the instruction or the program is not equivalent to that of a public school. This is illustrated by *Rice,* where deeply religious parents, who lacked the required professional qualifications to teach, refused to send their children to a public school "where they may be subjected to unwholesome influences." Consequently they were charged with a violation of the compulsory school attendance law and convicted accordingly. In support of its ruling the court stated:

. . . in order to impart an education to a child, it is self-evident that the instructor must himself have adequate learning and training in the art of teaching. Obviously, an illiterate parent cannot properly educate his child, nor can he, by attempting to do so, avoid his obligation to send his child to school. No amount of religious fervor he may entertain in opposition to adequate instruction should be allowed to work a life-long injury to his child. Nor should he for religious reasons, be suffered to inflict another illiterate citizen on his community or his state (*Id.* at 348).

3. *Stephens v. Bongart,* 15 N.J. Misc. 80, 189 A. 131 (1937).

Although compulsory school attendance requirements may sometimes be satisfied by home instruction — providing the home instruction is "equivalent" to that provided in a public school — it is frequently held in some jurisdictions that home instruction *cannot* be "equivalent" to that of public school instruction in social development of the child. For example, in *Stephens v. Bongart,* where parents instituted a program of home instruction in lieu of instruction provided by a public school, the court held that the home instruction program lacked the ability to develop attitudes and to create a proper social setting conducive to adequate social development. After referring to the great value of social training, Judge Siegler declared:

> I incline to the opinion that education is no longer concerned merely with the acquisition of facts; the instilling of worthy habits, attitudes, appreciations, and skills is far more important than mere imparting of subject-matter. A primary objective of education today is the development of character and good citizenship. Education must impart to the child the way to live. This brings me to the belief that, in a cosmopolitan area such as we live in, with all the complexities of life, and our reliance upon others to carry out the functions of education, it is almost impossible for a child to be adequately taught in the home. I cannot conceive how a child can receive in the home instruction and experiences and group activity

and a social outlook in any manner or form comparable to that provided in the public school (*Id.* at 137).

4. *Wisconsin v. Yoder,* 406 U.S. 205, 92 S. Ct. 1526, 32 L.Ed.2d 15 (1972).

This is the first case, involving compulsory school attendance requirements, to reach the United States Supreme Court. The constitutional question concerned whether Amish parents are exempt from the Wisconsin compulsory school attendance law in view of the Free Exercise Clause of the First Amendment because of their conflicting religious beliefs. Amish parents insisted that high school attendance laws are contrary to the Amish religion and way of life and that they "endanger their own salvation and that of their children by complying with the law."

The United States Supreme Court held that the First and Fourteenth Amendments prevent a state from compelling Amish parents to cause their children, who have graduated from the eighth grade, to attend formal high school to age sixteen. After hearing detailed testimony supporting the Amish religious principles described by experts of the Amish society, Chief Justice Burger delivered the opinion which stated in conclusion that:

> Aided by a history of three centuries as an identifiable religious sect and a long history as a successful and self-sufficient segment of American society, the Amish in this case have convincingly demonstrated the sincerity of their religious beliefs, the interrelationship of

13

belief with their mode of life, the vital role that belief and daily conduct play in the continued survival of Old Order Amish communities and their religious organization, and the hazards presented by the State's enforcement of a statute generally valid as to others. Beyond this, they have carried the even more difficult burden of demonstrating the adequacy of their alternative mode of continuing informal vocational education in terms of precisely those overall interests that the State advances in support of its program of compulsory high school education. In light of this convincing showing, one that probably few other religious groups or sects could make, and weighing the minimal difference between what the states would require and what the Amish already accept, it was incumbent on the State to show with more particularity how its admittedly strong interest in compulsory education would be adversely affected by granting an exemption to the Amish (*Id.* at 92 S. Ct. 1543).

Justice Douglas dissented with part of the majority opinion because he believed that the child should have a voice in his educational future. In voicing his dissent, he declared:

On this important and vital matter of education, I think the children should be entitled to be heard. While the parents, absent dissent, normally speak for the entire family, the education of the child is a matter on which the child will often have decided views. He may want to be a pianist, or an astronaut or an ocean geographer. To do so he will have to break from the Amish tradition.

It is the future of the student, not the future of the parents, that is imperilled in today's decision. If a parent keeps his child out of school beyond the grade school, then the child will be forever barred from entry into the new and amazing world of diversity that we have today. The child may decide that that is the preferred course, or he may rebel. It is the student's judgment, not his parents, that is essential if we are to give full meaning to what we have said about the Bill of Rights and of the right of students to be masters of their own destiny. If he is harnessed to the Amish way of life by those in authority over him and if his education is truncated, his entire life may be stunted and deformed. The child, therefore, should be given an opportunity to be heard from before the State gives exemption which we honor today. (*Id.* at 1547-48).

5. *Sheehan v. Scott,* 520 F.2d 825 (U.S.C.A. 7th Cir., 1975).

As indicated in this case, long and frequent absences are violative of the compulsory school attendance laws. The plaintiff's argument was that the state's right to compel school attendance is limited according to rulings in previous cases. The court, however, refused that argument and stated that:

In *Pierce* the court held a state statute void which required parents to send their children only to public schools. The court did not question the state's power to compel school attendance generally. Finally, in *Yoder* the court prefaced its discussion by stating that there is no doubt as to the power of a state to impose reasonable regulations for the control and duration of basic education but then went on to hold that the Old Order Amish could not be required to send their children to school beyond the eighth grade due to overriding principles of religious freedom. Such countervailing principles are not alleged in this case (*Id.* at 828).

Sporadic or occasional absence even though violative of the compulsory requirement of the law does not activate action under state statute here challenged. That is only triggered by habitual truancy. Plaintiff apparently is complaining that he is uncertain how many times he can violate the compulsory attendance requirement before effective action will be initiated against him. We decline to interfere with the reasonable judgmental discretion to be exercised by school authorities in defining exactly where the thin ice ends (*Id.* at 830).

§ 1.3 Vaccination as a condition for attendance.

1. *People v. Ekerold,* 211 N.Y. 386, 105 N.E. 670 (1914).

Courts generally hold that parents are guilty of violating the compulsory school attendance laws even when the children are sent to school but denied admission because of failure to meet vaccination requirements. For example, in this early case, the court based its decision on legislative intent rather than on strict construction of the statute. The court pointed out that it was readily apparent that the legislature, in passing one law requiring compulsory school attendance, and in passing another requiring vaccination as a condition for admission, did not intend that one should be used as an excuse to disobey the other. The rationale of the court follows:

> It is hardly to be assumed that when the Legislature passed the later statute there had slipped from its theoretical mind remembrance of the other law providing a very important condition of attendance at public schools, and, if it had purposed that a child might be excused from attendance by reason of the unwillingness of its parent to have it vaccinated, I cannot but believe that something would have been said on that subject.
>
> It does not require much spirit of prophecy to foresee what will follow a contrary construction of the statute. If a parent may escape all obligation under the statute requiring him to send his children to school by simply alleging that he does not believe in vaccination, the policy of the state to give some education to all children, if necessary by compelling measures, will become more or less a farce under existing legislation (*Id.* at 672).

2. *Anderson v. State,* 84 Ga. App. 259, 65 S.E.2d 848 (1951).

The majority of cases evolving from violation of the compulsory school attendance laws where vaccination is a mandated condition for attendance are based upon religious beliefs. For instance, in this case parents objected to the vaccination requirement because it was against their religious beliefs; they believed in divine healing through faith rather than taking vaccination or immunization against disease. The court, however, took a dim view of that argument and accordingly held the parents guilty for violating the compulsory school attendance law of the state and replied:

> Liberty of conscience is one thing. License to endanger the lives of others by practice contrary to statutes passed for the public safety and reliance upon modern medical knowledge is another. . . . The defendant in this case sought to comply with their duty to send their children to school but at the same time usurp the prerogative of the school authorities, and also undertook to fix the rules under which they should attend. Their contention therefore that they did actually enroll the children unvaccinated constitutes no valid defense. . . . Such a contention is unsound for the reason that an offer to do a thing only upon waiver of the conditions precedent thereto amounts to no offer at all (*Id.* at 852).

3. *In re Maria R.*, 366 N.Y.S.2d 309 (Family Court, City of N.Y. 1975).

There are instances where parents may be exempted from the vaccination requirement if there is positive proof that the parents are bona fide members of a religious organization, which forbids the use of vaccine. The actual issue in this case was whether the parents were guilty of neglect in that they failed to have their child vaccinated so that he might attend school.

In ruling for the parents, the court stated:

> Respondents are members of the Evangelic Appentecost Church. . . . It has been stipulated by Corporation Counsel, Bureau of Child Welfare and the attorneys for the parties that Respondents hold to the tenets of this religion and that this religion forbids and discourages the use of vaccines and other medical treatments. Respondents therefore claim an exemption from providing vaccination for their children pursuant to Section 2164(8) of the Public Health Law which states:
>
> "This section shall not apply to children whose parent, parents, or guardian are bona fide members of a recognized religious organization whose teachings are contrary to the practices herein required, and no certificate shall be required as a prerequisite to such children being admitted or received into school or attending school."
>
> It is the conclusion of this court that the parents hold bona fide religious beliefs which

forbid them to receive medical treatment and are entitled to the above exemption (*Id.* at 310).

§ 1.4 Attendance status of married girls.

1. *State v. Priest,* 210 La. 389, 27 So. 2d 173 (1946).

This is the first case, and also a precedential one, concerning the issue as to whether married girls could be *compelled* to attend school. Here a 15-year-old girl contested the legality of a school regulation and a juvenile court order to attend school.

When carried to the Louisiana Supreme Court, it was ruled that marriage "emancipates" a minor female and accordingly releases her from the compulsory school attendance laws. In refuting the claim that the marriage was unlawful due to violation of the legal age limits for marriage in Louisiana, the court responded:

> . . . such marriage once performed becomes a valid and legal marriage (if there are no legal impediments other than age), and that the female minor thus married enjoys the status of a wife and has a right to live at the matrimonial domicile of her husband and is no longer under the control of her parents (*Id.* at 174).

2. *In re State in Interest of Goodwin,* 214 La. 1062, 39 So. 2d 731 (1949).

The same issue, in the same state, with the same court ruling, was litigated in 1949. In this case a 14-year-old married girl disagreed with school authorities and a lower court order that her absence from school contributed to "truancy" in her case. The State

Supreme Court ruled for the girl on the grounds that she could not legally be required to attend school, by virtue of the fact that she was "irrevocably emancipated." As in the preceding case, the court disregarded the claim of an alleged under-age marriage and declared:

> Consequently, Clydell is irrevocably emancipated by this marriage as a matter of right. And although until she reaches the age of 18 she is not relieved of all the disabilities that attach to minority of this emancipation, she is relieved of parental control and, as was held in the Priest case, is no longer amenable to the compulsory school attendance law of this state . . . (*Id.* at 733).

3. *McLeod v. State,* 154 Miss. 468, 122 So. 737 (1929).

In direct contrast to those cases where school boards attempted to *compel* school attendance of married girls, there are cases in which school board regulations are designed to *prohibit* school attendance of married girls. Most noteworthy of the prohibitory cases is where a 15-year-old married girl was denied admission by school officials with the contention that "married students are detrimental to the good government and usefulness of the school." The court set aside this contention and ruled in favor of the girl. In support of its action the court made the following classic statement:

> It is argued that marriage emancipates a child from all parental control of its conduct, as well as such control by the school authorities; and that the marriage relation brings about

21

views of life which should not be known to unmarried children; that a married child in the public schools will make known to its associates in schools such views, which will therefore be detrimental to the welfare of the school. We fail to appreciate the force of the argument. Marriage is a domestic relation highly favored by law. When the relation is entered into with correct motives, the effect on the husband and wife is refining and elevating, rather than demoralizing. Pupils associating in school with a child occupying such a relation, it seems, would be benefited instead of harmed. And, furthermore, it is commendable in married persons of school age to desire to further pursue their education, and thereby become better fitted for the duties of life. And they are as much subject to the rules of the school as unmarried pupils, and punishable to the same extent for a breach of such rules. (*Id.* at 738-39).

4. *Nutt v. Board of Education of Goodland,* 128 Kan. 507, 278 P. 1065 (1928).

The same judicial reasoning as prevailed in *McLeod,* was expressed by a Kansas court in this case when it overturned the school board's refusal of readmission of a married girl who left school temporarily because she had previously given birth to a child conceived out of wedlock, but was married before the child was born. The court commented as follows:

The fact that the plaintiff's daughter desired to attend school was of itself an indication of character warranting favorable consideration. Other than the fact that she had a child conceived out of wedlock, no sufficient reason is advanced for preventing her from attending school. Her child was born in wedlock, and the fact that her husband may have abandoned her should not prevent her from gaining an education which would better fit her to meet the problems of life (*Id.* at 1066).

5. *Alvin Independent School District v. Cooper* (Tex. Civ. App.), 404 S.W.2d 76 (1966).

In this case a 16-year-old girl divorced her husband and sought readmission to the high school, which was denied by the school board in accordance with a board policy that:

A pupil who marries can no longer considered a youth. By the very act of getting married, he or she becomes an adult and assumes the responsibility of adulthood. . . . If a married pupil wants to start her family, she must withdraw from public school (*Id.* at 77).

In voiding the board's rule, the court stated:

The practical and legal effect is that appellee is deprived of a legal education, except as she might obtain it at her own expense in a private or parochial school. . . . We are of the view that appellants were without legal authority to

23

adopt the rule or policy that excludes the mother of a child from admission to the school if she is of the age for which the State furnishes school funds (*Id.* at 77).

§ 1.5 Attendance status of unwed pregnant students.

1. *Perry v. Grenada Municipal Separate School District,* 300 F. Supp. 748 (Miss. 1969).

In the first case brought before a federal court dealing with this issue, it was revealed that two young *unwed mothers* were denied high school admission by the school board. The court agreed with the girls' complaint that the school board's policy of excluding unwed mothers from high school admission violated the due process and equal protection clauses of the Fourteenth Amendment. The reasoning of the court's decision is stated in the following terms:

> Certainly school officials recognize the importance of education and the effect of a rigid rule which forever bars an individual from obtaining an education. . . .But after the girl has a child, she should have the opportunity for applying for re-admission and demonstrating to the school that she is qualified to continue her education. . . . Without a high school education, the individual is ill equipped for life, and is prevented from seeking higher education.
>
> The court would like to make manifestly clear that lack of moral character is certainly reason for excluding a child from public education. But the fact that the girl has one

child out of wedlock does not forever brand her
as a scarlet woman undeserving of any chance
for rehabilitation or the opportunity for future
education (*Id.* at 753).

2. *Ordway v. Hargraves,* 323 F. Supp. 1155 (Mass.
1971).

The attendance status of an *unwed pregnant* girl was
the subject of litigation when the high school principal
attempted to carry out a board policy which stipulated:
"Whenever an unmarried girl enrolled in North
Middlesex Regional High School shall be known to be
pregnant, her membership in the school shall be
immediately terminated" (*Id.* at 1156) (Mass. 1971).

When the pregnancy of the girl was detected she was
informed that she could no longer attend regular
classes, although she could make use of certain school
facilities after formal dismissal time.

After considering testimony as to the girl's physical
and mental condition, and the unharmful effect of her
presence in the classroom, the court ordered that she be
reinstated in her classes. The rationale of the court's
decision follows:

> In summary, no danger to petitioner's
> physical or mental health resultant from her
> attending classes during regular school hours
> has been shown; no likelihood that her
> presence will cause any disruption of or
> interference with school activities or pose a
> threat of harm to others has been shown, and
> no valid educational or other reason to justify
> her segregation and to require her to receive a

type of educational treatment which is not the equal of that given to all others in her class has been shown.

It would seem beyond argument that the right to receive a public school education is a basic personal right or liberty. Consequently, the burden of justifying any school rule or regulation limiting or terminating that right is on the school authorities . . . respondents have failed to carry this burden (*Id.* at 1158).

§ 1.6 Attendance and assignment discrimination because of race.

1. *Brown v. Board of Education,* 347 U.S. 483, 74 S. Ct. 686 (1954).

On May 17, 1954, one of the most spectacular and significant judicial decisions of the century was handed down, without dissent, by the United States Supreme Court.

The case had its beginning when the parents of Linda Brown, a Negro elementary pupil, challenged a school board's requirement that the girl had to attend a Negro school which was inferior to a white school and further in distance from her home. It was contended that segregation in and of itself causes inferiority and is thus a denial of due process and equal protection — to which the High Court agreed.

Chief Justice Warren delivered the unanimous opinion of the court, the thrust of which is expressed in the following excerpts:

... there are findings below that the Negro and white schools involved have been equalized, or are being equalized, with respect to buildings, curricula, qualifications and salaries of teachers, and other "tangible" factors. Our decision, therefore, cannot turn on merely a comparison of these tangible factors in the Negro and white schools involved in each of the cases. We must look instead to the effect of segregation itself in public education.

In approaching this problem, we cannot turn the clock back to 1868 when the Amendment was adopted, or even to 1896 when *Plessy v. Ferguson* was written. We must consider public education in the light of its full development and its present place in American life throughout the Nation. Only in this way can it be determined if segregation in public schools deprives these plaintiffs of the equal protection of the laws.

Today, education is perhaps the most important function of state and local governments. Compulsory school attendance laws and the great expenditures for education both demonstrate our recognition of the importance of education to our democratic society. It is required in the performance of our most basic public responsibilities, even service in the armed forces. It is the very foundation of good citizenship. Today it is a principal instrument in awakening the child to cultural values, in preparing him for later professional training and in helping him to adjust normally to his environment. In these days, it is doubtful that any child may reasonably be expected to succeed in life if he is denied the opportunity of an education. Such an opportunity, where the state has undertaken to provide it, is a right which must be available to all on equal terms.

We come then to the question presented. Does segregation of children in public schools solely on the basis of race, even though the physical facilities and other "tangible" factors may be equal, deprive the children of the minority group of equal educational opportunities? We believe that it does.

. . . A sense of inferiority affects the motivation of a child to learn. Segregation with the sanction of law, therefore, has a tendency to [retard] the educational and mental development of Negro children and to deprive them of the benefits they would receive in a racially integrated school system. Whatever may have been the extent of *Plessy v. Ferguson,* this finding is amply supported by modern authority. Any language by *Plessy v. Ferguson* contrary to this finding is rejected.

We conclude that in the field of public education the doctrine of "separate but equal" has no place. Separate educational facilities are inherently unequal. Therefore, we hold the plaintiffs and others similarly situated for whom the actions have been brought are, by reason of the segregation complained of, deprived of the equal protection of the laws guaranteed by the Fourteenth Amendment (347 U.S. 483, at 492-95).

2. *Cooper v. Aaron* (Ark.), 358 U.S. 1, 78 S. Ct. 1401 (1958).

Following the *Brown* decision there were numerous attempts to circumvent or defy the decision of the United States Supreme Court. The most noteworthy was that of *Cooper v. Aaron,* where the Legislature and Governor of the state of Arkansas defied the recommendations of the Little Rock School board, and actively pursued a program "designed to perpetuate in Arkansas the system of racial segregation which this Court had held violated the Fourteenth Amendment."

The forceful denunciation of the Arkansas official's action was expressed by Chief Justice Warren, speaking for a unanimous opinion:

No state legislator or executive or judicial officer can war against the Constitution without violating his understanding to support it. Chief Justice Marshall spoke for a unanimous Court in saying that: "If the legislatures of the several states may, at will, annul the judgments of the courts of the United States, and destroy the rights acquired under those judgments, the constitution itself becomes a mockery. . . ." A governor who asserts a power to nullify a federal court order is similarly restrained. If he had such power, said Chief Justice Hughes in 1932, also for a unanimous Court, "it is manifest that the fiat of a State Governor, and not the Constitution of the United States, would be the supreme power of the land; that the restrictions of the

Federal Constitution upon the exercise of state power would be but impotent phrases . . ." (358 U.S. 1, at 18).

In a concurring opinion Justice Frankfurter further stressed the gravity of the situation such as was evidenced at Little Rock:

The use of force to further obedience to law is in any event a last resort and one not congenial to the spirit of our Nation. But the tragic aspect of this disruptive tactic was that the power of the State was used not to sanction law but as an instrument for thwarting law. The State of Arkansas is thus responsible for disabling one of its subordinate agencies, the Little Rock School Board, from peacefully carrying out the Board's and State's constitutional duty. . . . Violent resistance to law cannot be made a legal reason for its suspension without loosening the fabric of our society. What could this mean but to acknowledge that disorder under the aegis of a State has moral superiority over the law of the Constitution? For those in authority thus to defy the law of the land is profoundly subversive not only of our constitutional system but of the presuppositions of a democratic society (*Id.* at 21-2).
. . . Compliance with decisions of this Court, as the constitutional organ of the Supreme Law of the Land, has often throughout our history, depended on active support by state and local authorities. It presupposes such

support. To withhold it, and indeed to use political power to try to paralyze the Supreme Law, precludes the maintenance of our federal system as we have known and cherished it for one hundred and seventy years (*Id.* at 26).

3. *Swann   v.   Charlotte-Mecklenburg   Board   of Education* (N.C.), 402 U.S. 1, 91 S. Ct. 1267 (1971).

The issue in this case is whether busing of students is a legitimate means of assignment and a constitutional desegregation tool to dismantle the dual school system.

The United States Supreme Court elucidated on four problem areas existing on the issue of student assignment but gave special emphasis to *transportation of students* which was the main area of contention in the case. Abbreviated portions of the complete court opinion are quoted as follows:

School authorities are traditionally charged with broad power to formulate and implement educational policy and might well conclude, for example, that in order to prepare students to live in a pluralistic society each school should have a prescribed ratio of Negro to white students reflecting the proportion for the district as a whole. To do this as an educational policy is within the broad discretionary powers of school authorities; absent a finding of a constitutional violation, however, that would not be within the authority of a federal court. As with any equity case, the nature of the violation determines the scope of the remedy. In default by the school authorities of their obligation to proffer acceptable remedies, a district court has broad power to fashion a remedy that will assure a unitary school system (402 U.S. 1, at 16).

The scope of permissible transportation of students as an implement of a remedial decree has never been defined by the Court and by the very nature of the problem it cannot be defined with precision. No rigid guidelines as to student transportation can be given for application to the infinite variety of problems presented in thousands of situations. Bus transportation has been an integral part of the public education system for years, and was perhaps the single most important factor in the transition from the one-room schoolhouse to the consolidated school. Eighteen million of the Nation's public school children, approximately 39%, were transported to their schools by bus in 1969-1970 in all parts of the country (*Id.* at 29).

An objection to transportation of students may have validity when the time or distance of travel is so great as to either risk the health of the children or significantly impinge on the educational process. District courts must weigh the soundness of any transportation plan. . . . It hardly needs stating that the limits on time of travel will vary with many factors, but probably with none more than the age of the students. The reconciliation of competing values in a desegregation case is, of course, a difficult task with many sensitive facets but fundamentally no more than remedial measure courts of equity have traditionally employed. (*Id.* at 30-31).

§ 1.7 Attendance and assignment discrimination because of sex.

1. *Vorcheimer v. School District of Philadelphia,* 400 F. Supp. 326 (E.D. Pa. 1975).

In this case a female high school student was successful in her suit against the school board, to be admitted to an academically superior boys' school, even though Philadelphia had a similar school for girls.

After reviewing the case from many angles and drawing from the United States Supreme Court decisions on related matters, the court finally held for the girl, and offered its rationale for doing so in the following words:

> Simply put, if coeducation is detrimental to girls, all the public schools should be sex-segregated; if it is not, then there is no "fair and substantial" relationship between sex-segregation and the educational goals of the School Board. The fundamental inconsistency which would result if the School Board argues that it keeps girls out of Central for their own protection reveals that males, and not females, are intended beneficiaries of the defendants' exclusionary policy (*Id.* at 342).

The court concluded by stating: "Defendants are enjoined from refusing to admit plaintiff or any other member of the class she represents to Central High School solely on the basis of sex" (*Id.* at 343).

Chapter 2

AUTHORITY OVER CURRICULAR ACTIVITIES

§ 2.1 Prescriptions of certain subjects.

The basic authority of the state to govern the public schools is embodied in the various state constitutions. The primary avenue through which that authority is expressed, however, is the state legislature. In fact, the state constitution usually charges the legislature with the responsibility for providing a state educational system, and accordingly grants the necessary authority to do so. Therefore, within the constitutional limits, *the legislature is empowered to determine the types and contents of curricula, and the manner of their control.*

In rare instances, the state constitutions provide for specific inclusions in the curriculum; but usually the state legislatures assume the power and responsibility. Consequently most states have enacted legislation requiring certain subject matter to be included in the public school curriculum. Frequently the statutory requirements are objectionable to some parents — even leading to the point of litigation. The following court cases alluded to in this chapter are illustrative:

1. *School Board District No. 18 v. Thompson,* 24 Okla. 1, 103 P. 578 (1909).

This early case refers to parental versus school authority over prescribed curricular issues. Here the

parents succeeded by mandamus action to compel
school authorities to reinstate their children in the
public schools, from which they were expelled for their
refusal, at their parents' direction, to take singing
lessons, which constituted part of the prescribed course
of study. The court held for the parents, and
emphasized the limited authority of school officials in
curricular prescriptions:

> To our mind the right of the board of
> education to prescribe the course of study and
> designate the text-books to be used does not
> carry with it the absolute power to require the
> pupils to study all of the branches prescribed
> in the course in opposition to the parents'
> reasonable wishes in relation to some of them
> (*Id.* at 579).

> The school authorities of the state have the
> power to classify and grade the scholars in
> their respective districts and cause them to be
> taught in such departments as they may deem
> expedient. They may also prescribe the courses
> of study and text-books for the use of the
> schools, and such reasonable rules and
> regulations as they may think needful. They
> may also require prompt attendance,
> respectful deportment, and diligence in study.
> The parent, however, has a right to make a
> reasonable selection from the prescribed
> course of study for his child to pursue, as the
> right of the parent in that regard is superior to
> that of school officers and the teacher (*Id.* at
> 582).

2. *Kelley v. Ferguson,* 95 Neb. 63, 144 N.W. 1039 (1914).

In another early case, denoting the school board's limited authority over the curriculum, the Nebraska Supreme Court ruled against a school board which refused a request of a parent to excuse his daughter from studying domestic science. In support of its ruling the court stated:

> The public school is one of the main bulwarks of our nation, and we would not knowingly do anything to undermine it; but we should be careful to avoid permitting our love for this noble institution to cause us to regard it as "all in all" and destroy both the God-given and constitutional right of a parent to have some voice in the bringing up and education of his children (*Id.* at 1043).
>
> The state is more and more taking hold of the private affairs of individuals and requiring that they conduct their business affairs honestly and with due regard for the public good. All this is very commendable and must receive sanction of every good citizen. But in this age of agitation, such as the world has never known before, we want to be careful lest we carry the doctrine of governmental paternalism too far, for after all is said and done, the prime factor in our scheme of government is the American home (*Id.* at 1044).

3. *Hardwick v. Board of Trustees,* 54 Cal. App. 696, 205 P. 49 (1921).

In this case it was revealed that parents requested their children to be excused from dancing as a part of physical education on the grounds that "such exercise was offensive to the conscientious scruples and contrary to the religious beliefs and principles" of the children and their parents. They were particularly opposed to those dances "where the arms of the children, as they danced with the opposite sex, were clasped around and above the shoulders of their dancing partners."

The request of the parents was denied and the pupils expelled because of refusal to participate. Although the court held the school authorities had no right to expel the children for their refusal to take part in the dancing the court upheld the right of the schools to include dancing in the curriculum. A brief excerpt of the court's rather lengthy discourse on the case follows:

> To the end that the public school system may in full measure function according to its purposes, there must, of course, be rules and regulations for the government thereof, and these the Legislature has either directly provided or has vested the school authorities with plenary power to establish and, quite naturally and with eminent propriety, has committed to said authorities the right and power to prescribe the courses of study to be followed in the various grades of the system and to maintain at all times the discipline indispensably necessary to the successful prosecution of the high purposes thereof. . . (*Id.* at 51).

4. *Mitchell v. McCall,* 273 Ala. 604, 143 So.2d 629, (1962).

Here a girl refused to engage in the activities of the prescribed physical education class because the costumes were, in her opinion, "immodest and sinful." The girl's father contended that the wearing of different clothes than those prescribed would make his daughter stand out as a "speckled bird" and "subject to the contumely of her fellow students."

In response to this contention the court stated:

> All citizens insofar as they hold views different from the majority of their fellows are subject to such inconveniences. And this is especially true of those who hold religious or moral beliefs which are looked upon with disdain by the majority. It is precisely every citizen's right to be a "speckled bird" that our constitutions, state and federal, seek to insure. And solace for the embarrassment that is attendant upon holding such beliefs must be found by the individual citizen in his own moral courage and strength of conviction, and not in a court of law (*Id.* at 632).

5. *Ovimette v. Babbie,* 405 F. Supp. 525 (D. Vt. 1975).

This case also involved the refusal of a girl to pursue a required course in physical education. The refusal in the instant case, however, was not because of *religious scruples,* but rather because of *obstinence.* According to the case report:

With the opening of the school year 1975-76 Yvonne attended all regularly scheduled classes except physical education. She is a determined young lady and has persistently refused to attend these classes. She announced that she would refuse to participate in the physical education program at any time in the future. . . . The only reason advanced by Yvonne was that she didn't like the course and that she preferred to spend her time in pursuit of academic studies. Yvonne won the support of her father in her persistent refusal to attend the physical education classes. He entertained a philosophical reason against compelling his daughter to attend classes against her choice (*Id.* at 526).

The principal "informed the student that she would be denied admission to school if she elected to remain away from her class in physical education." Since the warning was unheeded, she was suspended.

In upholding the resulting suspension, the court held the school authorities' action "was not unreasonable, arbitrary or capricious," and added:

As long as the prescribed courses of study do not trench on fundamental rights guaranteed by the paramount law, the plaintiff's personal conflict with the defendants is beyond the court's reach . . . courts consistently have affirmed the curriculum controls belong to the political process and local school authorities (*Id.* at 530).

§ 2.2 Restrictive attempts against instruction of certain subjects.

1. *Meyer v. Nebraska,* 262 U.S. 390, 43 S. Ct. 625 (1923).

The issue in this case concerned the validity of a state statute forbidding the teaching of modern languages in any school, public, private or parochial, to any child who had not completed the eighth grade. The main factor leading up to the case indicates that, after World War I, several states enacted legislation prohibiting the teaching of German to nonpublic or public school pupils who had not completed requirements of the eighth grade.

Although the courts of three states (Nebraska, Iowa, and Ohio) had sanctioned the legislation as legitimate exercise of police power, the United States Supreme Court ruled that the legislation was an arbitrary interference with the liberty of parents to control and educate their children, and that it violated the liberty guaranteed by the Fourteenth Amendment. The following excerpt indicates the court's reasoning in its decision:

> It is said the purpose of the legislation was to promote civic development by inhibiting training and education of the immature in foreign tongue and ideals before they could learn English and acquire American ideals; and that the English language should be and become the mother tongue of all children reared in this State. It is also affirmed that the foreign born population is very large, that

certain communities commonly use foreign
words, follow foreign leaders, move in a
foreign atmosphere, and that children are
thereby hindered from becoming citizens of
the most useful type and the public safety is
imperiled.

That the State may do much, go very far,
indeed, in order to improve the quality of its
citizens, physically, mentally and morally, is
clear; but the individual has certain
fundamental rights which must be respected.
The protection of the Constitution extends to
all, to those who speak other languages as well
as those born with English on the tongue.
Perhaps it would be highly advantageous if all
had ready understanding of our ordinary
speech, but this cannot be coerced by methods
which conflict with the Constitution — a
desirable end cannot be promoted by
prohibited means (262 U.S. 390 at 402).

2. *Epperson v. Arkansas,* 393 U.S. 97, 89 S. Ct. 266
(1968).

The issue in this case pertains to the constitutionality
of an Arkansas "anti-evolution" law which prohibits the
teaching in its public schools the theory that man
evolved from other species of life.

A teacher (Susan Epperson) sought a declaration
against the State that the statute was void, and to keep
defendant officials from dismissing her for violation of
the statute which aimed to prohibit the teaching of
evolution. The Supreme Court of Arkansas upheld the

statute on the grounds that it constituted "an exercise of the State's power to specify the curriculum in public schools."

The United States Supreme Court, however, reversed the State Court decision and unanimously declared the Arkansas statute to be unconstitutional on the narrow grounds of the First Amendment's Establishment of Religion clause.

Justice Fortas, who delivered the opinion of the court, emphasized that:

> The State's undoubted right to prescribe the curriculum for its public schools does not carry with it the right to prohibit, on pain of criminal penalty, the teaching of a scientific theory or doctrine where that prohibition is based upon reasons that violate the First Amendment. It is much too late to argue that the State may impose upon the teacher in its schools any conditions that it chooses, however restrictive they may be of constitutional guarantees. . . .
>
> In the present case, there can be no doubt that Arkansas has sought to prevent its teachers from discussing the theory of evolution because it is contrary to the belief of some that the Book of Genesis must be the exclusive source of doctrine as to the origin of man. No suggestion has been made that Arkansas' law may be justified by consideration of state policy other than the religious views of some of its citizens. It is clear that fundamental sectarian conviction

43

was and is the law's reason for existence. Its antecedent, Tennessee's "monkey law" candidly stated its purpose: to make it unlawful "to teach any theory that denies the story of Divine Creation of man as taught in the Bible, and to teach instead that man has descended from a lower order of animals." Perhaps the sensational publicity attendant upon the *Scopes* trial induced Arkansas to adopt less explicit language. It eliminated Tennessee's reference to "the story of the Divine Creation of man" as taught in the Bible, but there is no doubt that the motivation for the law was the same: to suppress the teaching of a theory which it was thought "denied" the divine creation of man.

Arkansas law cannot be defended as an act of religious neutrality. Arkansas did not seek to excuse from the curricula of its schools and universities all discussion of the origin of man. The law's effort was confined to an attempt to blot out a particular theory because of its supposed conflict with the Biblical account, literally read. Plainly, the law is contrary to the mandate of the First, and in violation of the Fourteenth Amendment to the Constitution (393 U.S. 97, at 107-09).

3. *Wright v. Houston Independent School District,* 486 F.2d 137 (U.S.C.A. Fifth Circuit 1973).

In this case, plaintiffs sought to enjoin the Houston Independent School District from teaching the *theory of evolution,* without teaching the other theories regarding human origin. They contended that the study of evolution in the school's curriculum "constitutes the establishment of a sectarian, atheistic religion" in violation of the First Amendment. To this contention the court responded as follows:

> Contrary to the concise, able, and vigorous arguments of plaintiffs, the Federal courts cannot by judicial decree do that which the Supreme Court has declared the state legislatures powerless to do, *i.e.,* prevent teaching the theory of evolution in public school for religious reasons (*Epperson*). To require the teaching of every theory of human origin, as alternatively suggested by plaintiffs, would be an unwarranted intrusion into the authority of public school systems to control the academic curriculum (*Id.* at 138).

4. *Steele v. Waters,* 527 S.W.2d 72 (Tenn. 1975).

In this case, invloving text-book reference to evolution, the Supreme Court of Tennessee held that a state statute, which requires:

> .... textbooks to state that such theory is not represented as scientific fact and that such books are to give equal emphasis to the origin and creation as the same is recorded in other theories, including, but not limited to the Genesis account in the Bible and that teaching of all occult or satanical beliefs of human origin is excluded violates both the Federal and State Constitutions (*Id.* at 72).

Throughout human history the God of some men has frequently been regarded as the Devil incarnate by man of other religious persuasions. It would be utterly impossible for the Textbook Commission to determine which religious theories were "occult" or "satanical" without seeking to resolve the theologians through the ages.

The requirement that some religious concepts of creation, adhered to presumably by some Tennessee citizens, be excluded on such grounds in favor of the Bible of the Jews and the Christians represents still another method of preferential treatment of particular faiths by state law and, of course, is forbidden by the establishment clause of the First Amendment (*Id.* at 73).

5. *Cornwell v. State Board of Education,* 314 F. Supp. 340 (Md. 1969).

Parents frequently object to having *sex education* included in the public school curriculum. For example, in this case which was adjudicated at the United States District Court level, where a by-law of the Maryland State Board of Education was challenged. The provision of the by-law was as follows:

It is the responsibility of the local school system to provide a comprehensive program of family life and sex education in every elementary and secondary school for all students as an integral part of the curriculum including a planned sequential program of health education (*Id.* at 341).

In response to the plaintiff's contention that the by-law denied equal protection of the law, the court responded:

> Assuredly it cannot be said that the by-law here is arbitrary or unreasonable exercise of the authority vested in the State Board to determine a teaching curriculum, nor that there is no basis in fact for the legislative policy expressed in the by-law. Furthermore, it does not appear that the by-law denies equal protection of the laws, as on its face it applies to all pupils equally.
>
> The plaintiff's argument that the by-law is defective because it applies to non-pregnant as well as pregnant people is difficult to follow. There would appear to be just as much reason for the State Board to provide sex education for the non-pregnant (and, incidentally, for the non-impregnating) or for those students who, because of a lack of information on the subject (as for other reasons) have become pregnant or who had caused pregnancy (*Id.* at 342).

6. *Hopkins v. Hamden Board of Education,* 289 A.2d 914, 29 CS397 (Conn. 1971).

Here the State Board of Education authorized a mandatory health education course which included sex education and family life.

Some parents, particularly those of Catholic religious faith, objected to the course to be included in the curriculum. The Catholic point of view was that "their religious beliefs imposed upon parents the primary obligations for education of their children and that, in the area of sexual education particularly, papal enclicals and Vatican II directed parents to instruct their children in the home in sexual matters" (*Id.* at 920).

An excerpt of the court's opinion follows:

> The court is compelled to conclude under the facts in this case that there appears to be no denial of equal protection or substantive due process or equality under the Fourteenth Amendment, since the course is taught to all pupils, of mixed religious beliefs, and without discrimination. No evidence has been offered nor authority cited by the plaintiffs for their claim that the exclusive constitutional right to teach sexual matters exists only in the home and is therefore prohibited in the schools. Unless the plaintiffs claim that a secular program was a form of religion, there appears to be no proof, from evaluating the evidence in the light most favorably to the plaintiffs, that the teaching of the curriculum will in fact establish any religious concept or philosophy in the school system (*Id.* at 921-22).

7. *Medeiros v. Kiyosaki,* 478 P.2d 314 (Hawaii 1970).

In this case, parents and children challenged the constitutionality of showing film as part of a newly adopted program for family life and sex education. They questioned "whether parents are free to educate their offspring in the intimacies of sexual matters according to their own moral and religious beliefs without due interference by the State (*Id.* at 315).

School authorities injected an "excusal system" into the program whereby parents had the option of withholding or withdrawing their children from the program by submitting a written excuse to the school.

In holding that the plaintiff's right of privacy was not violated, the court said:

> We view the "excusal system" as an effort by the defendants to allow those parents or guardians who might object to the Program or parts thereof on moral and religious grounds to have their children excused. The program was in no way compulsory, and, therefore, we cannot see how the State by (unnecessarily broad means) contravened plaintiffs' right of privacy (*Id.* at 317).

8. *Hobolth v. Greenway,* 52 Mich. App. 682, 218 N.W.2d 98 (1974).

Here again parents objected to a sex education course in the curriculum. The purposes of the course were well defined. It also provided for an "excusal system."

When carried to the Court of Appeals of Michigan, that court upheld the sex education program and concluded with the following remark:

> Neither the establishment of a course of instruction on sex education nor attendance at such a course, if established, is compulsory. The board of education can establish the course if it wishes. If established, a student can take the course if he desires and is authorized to do so by a parent or parents. (*Id.* at 100).

9. *Citizens for Parental Rights v. San Mateo County Board of Education,* 51 Cal. App. 3d 1, 124 Cal. Rptr. 68 (Ct. of Ap. First District, Div. 2, 1975).

At the time of this writing, this is the last case reported concerning the legality of including *sex education* in the public school curriculum. It arose as an action against the county for declaratory and injunctive relief against teaching of family life and sex education in several school districts. A Superior Court *dismissed* the complaint, stating that:

. . . in view of parents' statutory right to remove their children from all or any portion of the courses of instruction, the courses of instruction did not impair free exercise of religion of the parents and their students; that the courses of instruction did not represent the establishment of religion; that the exclusionary provisions did not violate equal protection or due process; and that courses of instruction did not violate parents' or students' rights to life, liberty and the pursuit of happiness, as guaranteed by State Constitution, nor usurp parental control (*Id.* at 68).

The parents appealed to the Court of Appeals, where the ruling of the Superior Court was affirmed as indicated by its concluding statement:

We conclude, therefore, that the trial court properly concluded that, accepting the various allegations of the complaint to be true, the parents have failed to raise any substantial constitutional issues or any factual issues that would entitle them to the declaratory or injunctive relief sought. Accordingly, the county's motion to dismiss the entire complaint was properly granted and the judgment appealed from is affirmed (*Id.* at 92).

§ 2.3 Regulations concerning loyalty display.

1. *Minersville School District v. Gobitis* (Pa.), 310 U.S. 586, 60 S. Ct. 1010 (1940).

As early as 1937, cases involving the authority of schools to require, as a part of the school program, students to *salute the flag of the United States and take the oath of allegiance* confronted the state courts. In virtually all early instances, the state courts upheld the legality of the requirement. Even the United States Supreme Court did likewise as indicated in the case cited above.

Justice Frankfurter, who expressed trepidation in taking the case, delivered the majority opinion of the court in these words:

The preciousness of the family relation, the authority and independence which give dignity to parenthood, indeed the enjoyment of all freedom, presuppose the kind of ordered society which is summarized by our flag. A society which is dedicated to the preservation of these ultimate values of civilization may in self-protection utilize the educational process for inculcating those almost unconscious feelings which bind men together in a comprehending loyalty, whatever may be their lesser differences and difficulties ... (310 U.S. 586 at 600).

In his strong dissent, Justice Stone stated, in part:

The Constitution expresses more than the conviction of the people that democratic processes must be preserved at all costs. It is also an expression of faith and a command that freedom of mind and spirit must be preserved, which government must obey, if it is to adhere to that justice and moderation without which no free government can exist. For this reason it would seem that legislation which operates to repress the religious freedom of small minorities, which is admittedly within the scope of the protection of the Bill of Rights, must at least be subject to the same judicial scrutiny as legislation which we have recently held to infringe the constitutional liberty of religious and racial minorities.

With such scrutiny, I cannot say that the inconveniences which may attend some sensible adjustment of school discipline in order that the religious convictions of these children may be spared, presents a problem so momentous or pressing as to outweigh the freedom from compulsory violation of religious faith which has been thought worthy of constitutional protection (*Id.* at 606-7).

2. *West Virginia State Board of Education v. Barnette*, 319 U.S. 624, 63 S. Ct. 1178 (1943).

The issue in this case was quite similar to that involved in the preceding case *(Gobitis)* in that it mentioned the validity of a requirement for children to salute the American flag who claimed religious scruples against doing so.

In its decision the United States Supreme Court ruled that the rule requiring all students to salute the flag and recite the pledge of allegiance thereto as a condition of school attendance violated the First Amendment to the Federal Constitution which guarantees the exercise of freedom of religion.

Noteworthy, in the majority and dissenting opinions, are some brief excerpts written by Justices Jackson and Frankfurter. Justice Jackson, speaking for the majority, remarked;

> If there is any fixed star in our constellation, it is that no official, high or petty, can prescribe what shall be orthodox in politics, nationalism, religion, or other matters of opinion or force citizens to confess by word or act their faith therein. If there are any circumstances which permit an exemption, they do not now occur to us.

> We think the action of the local authorities in compelling the flag salute and pledge transcends constitutional limitations on their power and invades the sphere of intellect and spirit which it is the purpose of the First Amendment to our Constitution to reserve from all official control (319 U.S. 624, at 640-42).

Justice Frankfurter was just as forceful in stating his
dissent in the case *(Barnette)* as he was in speaking for
the majority on the preceding case *(Gobitis)*. A brief
excerpt of his dissent follows:

> We are told that a flag salute is a doubtful
> substitute for adequate understanding of our
> institutions. The states that require such a
> school exercise do not have to justify it as the
> only means for promoting good citizenship in
> children, but merely as one of diverse means
> for accomplishing a worthy end. We may deem
> it a foolish measure, but the point is that this
> Court is not the organ of government to
> resolve doubts as to whether it will fulfill its
> purpose. Only if there be no doubt that any
> reasonable mind could entertain can we deny
> to the states the right to resolve doubts their
> way and not ours.
>
> That which to the majority may seem
> essential for the welfare of the state may
> offend the consciences of a minority. But, so
> long as no inroads are made upon the actual
> exercise of religion by the minority, to deny the
> political power of the majority to enact laws
> concerned with civil matters, simply because
> they may offend the consciences of a minority,
> really means that the consciences of a minority
> are more sacred and more enshrined in the
> Constitution than the consciences of a majority
> (*Id.* at 661-62).

3. *Holden v. Board of Education of Elizabeth,* 46 N.J.
279, 216 A.2d 387 (1966).

The flag salute issue has been adjudicated in state courts several times since the *Barnette* decision. In general, the state courts have followed the legal precedent established in the last United States Supreme Court ruling.

For example, in 1966, the Supreme Court of New Jersey ordered a school board to reinstate children who had been excluded from school because of their refusal to salute the flag of the United States. Their refusal was based upon their religion (Black Muslims) where they taught that "their sole allegiance was to Almighty God Allah and that the flag was but a symbol, it would be contrary to their teachings to pledge allegiance to any flag...."

In holding for plaintiff parents, the court stated that

> ... all who live under the protection of our flag are free to believe whatever thay may choose to believe and to express that belief, within the limits of free expression, no matter how unfounded or ludicrous the professed belief may seem to others.... The teachings are such as to cause children not to participate in a common ceremony to the Flag, which is itself the emblem of those freedoms which all Americans are privileged to enjoy.... Those freedoms, as contemplated by Federal and State Constitutions and by State law, are broad enough to encompass the beliefs of those who, like the petitioner, claim conscientious scruples (*Id.* at 391).

4. *Frain v. Baron,* 307 F. Supp. 27 (U.S.D.C. E.D.N.Y. 1969).

Likewise it was held by a federal court that a student could not be excluded from the classroom during the pledge of allegiance merely "for reasons of conscience to participate in the Pledge in any different way from those who participate." The court added:

> The original concern with limitation of the state's power to compel a student to act contrary to his beliefs has shifted to a concern for affirmative protection of a student's right to express his beliefs. The present case is novel in that the context, school patriotic exercises, is one in which courts have previously intervened to limit coerced participation, while these plaintiffs are urging not only a right of nonparticipation but a right of silent protest by remaining seated (*Id.* at 30-31).
>
> ... The student is free to select his form of expression, so long as he does not materially infringe the rights of other students or disrupt school activities (*Id.* at 32).

5. *Banks v. Board of Public Instruction of Dade County*, 314 F. Supp. 285 (U.S.D.C. 1970).

Similarly it was ruled by a United States District Court that a student could not be legally suspended from school as a result of his refusal to stand during the pledge of allegiance. The court stated:

> The right to differ and express one's opinions, to fully vent his First Amendment rights, even to the extent of exhibiting disrespect for our flag and country by refusing to stand and participate in the pledge of allegiance, cannot be suppressed by the imposition of suspension (*Id.* at 286).

56

6. *Goetz v. Ansell*, 477 F.2d 636 (C.A.N.Y. 1973).

The plaintiff (Goetz) who was a senior, an honor student and president of his class, refused "to participate in the Pledge of Allegiance because he believes that there [isn't] liberty and justice for all in the United States" (*Id.* at 636).

In holding for the student, the court stated:

> There is no evidence here of disruption of classwork or disorder or invasion of the rights of others. The record is just to the contrary. . . .
>
> While we do not share plaintiff's resistance to pledging allegiance to this nation, his reservations of belief must be protected. In time, perhaps, he will recognize that such protection is sound ground for a firmer trust in his country (*Id.* at 638-39).

§ 2.4 Regulations concerning religious instruction.

Very few curriculum issues, if any, concerning disputes between parents and schools have been litigated more often than that of pupil participation in religious exercises. Required reading of passages from the Bible and recitation of prayers have been most vigorously disputed and litigated of the various religious exercises in public schools.

1. *Doremus v. Board of Education*, 5 N.J. 435, 75 A.2d 880 (1950); 342 U.S. 429 (1952).

In this case, certain parents brought action against the school board and the state to test the constitutionality of a statute which provided that "at least five verses taken from that portion of the Holy Bible known as the Old Testament shall be read, or caused to be read, without comment, in each public school classroom."

The Supreme Court of New Jersey disagreed with allegations that the statute violated the First and Fourteenth Amendments which prohibit the intermingling of religious and secular education in the public schools. It not only upheld the constitutionality of the disputed statute but commented on its appropriateness and timeliness in the following manner:

> While it is necessary that there be a separation between church and state, it is not necessary that the state should be stripped of religious sentiment. It may be a tragic experience for this country and for its conception of life, liberty and the pursuit of happiness if our people lose their religious feeling and are left to live their lives without faith. . . . We are at a crucial hour in which it may behoove our people to conserve all of the elements which have made our land what it is. Faced with this threat to the continuance of elements deeply imbedded in our national life the adoption of a public policy with respect thereto is a reasonable function to be performed by those on whom responsibility lies (*Id.* at 888).

The case was appealed to the United States Supreme Court where, in a six to three decision, the decision of the state court was affirmed.

2. *Abington School District v. Schempp* (Pa.), 374 U.S. 203, 83 S. Ct. 1560 (1963).

The issue in this case was whether a state law or school board may constitutionally require that passages of the Bible be read or that the Lord's Prayer be recited in the public schools—even if individual students may be excused from attending or participating in such exercises upon written request of their parents.

The Schempp family (Unitarians) brought suit to enjoin enforcement of the statute, contending that "their rights under the Fourteenth Amendment to the United States Constitution are, have been, and will continue to be violated unless this statute be declared unconstitutional or violative of these provisions of the First Amendment" (274 U.S. at 205).

The High Court agreed with the contention and placed stress and confirmation upon the following comment of the trial court:

> The reading of the verses, even without comment, possesses a devotional and religious character and constitutes in effect a religious observance. The devotional and religious nature of the morning exercise is made all the more apparent by the fact that the Bible reading is followed immediately by a recital in unison by the pupils of the Lord's Prayer. The fact that some pupils, or theoretically all pupils, might be excused from attendance as the exercises does not mitigate the obligatory nature of the ceremony.... The exercises are held in the school buildings and perforce are conducted by and under the authority of the local school authorities and during school sessions. Since the statute requires the reading

of the "Holy Bible" a Christian document, the practice ... prefers the Christian religion (*Id.* at 210-11).

Justice Stewart, the lone dissenter, refuted arguments of the majority by emphasizing that:

It might also be argued that parents who want their children exposed to religious influences can adequately fulfil that wish off school property and outside school time. With all its surface persuasiveness, however, this argument seriously misconceives the basic constitutional justification for permitting the exercises at issue in these cases. For a compulsory state educational system so structures a child's life that if religious exercises are held to be an impermissible activity in schools, religion is placed at an artificial and state-created disadvantage. Viewed in this light, permission of such exercises for those who want them is necessary if the schools are truly to be neutral in the matter of religion. And a refusal to permit religious exercises thus is seen, not as the realization of state neutrality, but rather as the establishment of a religion of secularism, or at the least, as government support of the beliefs of those who think that religious exercises should be conducted only in private (*Id.* at 313).

3. *Engel v. Vitale* (N.Y.), 370 U.S. 421, 82 S. Ct. 1261 (1962).

The issue here was whether state officials may constitutionally compose an official prayer and require that it be recited in the public schools of the State at the beginning of each school day—even if the prayer is denominationally neutral and if pupils who wish to do so may remain silent or be excused from the room while the prayer is being recited.

The brief prayer under contention reads as follows: "Almighty God, we acknowledge our dependence upon Thee, and we beg Thy blessing upon us, our parents, our teachers and our Country." Despite its brevity, the United States Supreme Court ruled that the requirement of the state-composed prayer in the public school classroom was in violation of the Establishment Clause of the First Amendment. In speaking for the majority Justice Black stated:

> We think that by using its public school system to encourage recitation of the Regents' prayer, the State of New York has adopted a practice wholly inconsistent with the Establishment Clause. There can, of course, be no doubt that New York's program of daily classroom invocation of God's blessings as prescribed in the Regents' prayer is a religious activity. It is a solemn avowal of divine faith and supplication for the blessings of the Almighty. The nature of such a prayer has always been religious . . . (370 U.S. at 424).
>
> It is a matter of history that this very practice of establishing governmentally composed prayers for religious services was one of the reasons which caused many of our

early colonists to leave England and seek religious freedom in America ... (*Id.* at 425).

In supporting the ruling of the court, Justice Black concluded by quoting the following passage from James Madison, the author of the First Amendment:

It is proper to take alarm at the first experiment on our liberties. ... Who does not see that the same authority which can establish Christianity, in exclusion of all other Religions, may establish with the same care any particular sect of Christians, in exclusion of all other Sects? That the same authority which can force a citizen to contribute three pence only of his property for the support of any one establishment, may force him to conform to any other's establishment in all cases whatsoever (*Id.* at 436).

Justice Stewart filed a dissent, part of which follows:

With all respect, I think the Court has misapplied a great constitutional principle. I cannot see how an "official religion" is established by letting those who want to say a prayer say it. On the contrary, I think that to deny the wish of these school children to join in reciting this prayer is to deny them the opportunity of sharing in the spiritual heritage of our Nation (*Id.* at 445).

I do not believe that this Court, or the Congress, or the President has by the actions and practices I have mentioned established an "official religion" in violation of the

Constitution. And I do not believe the State of New York has done so in this case. What each has done has been to recognize and to follow the deeply entrenched and highly cherished spiritual traditions of our Nation—traditions which come down to us from those who almost two hundred years ago avowed their "firm Reliance on the Protection of divine Providence," when they proclaimed the freedom and independence of this brave new world (*Id.* at 450).

4. *DeSpain v. DeKalb Community School District* (Ill.), 384 F.2d 836 (U.S.C.A. 7th Cir., 1968).

The force of the *Engel* decision can be seen in this case where a federal court held that a recitation of a verse (prayer) by children in a kindergarten class before their morning snack was unconstitutional. The verse read:

> We thank you for the flowers so sweet;
> We thank you for the food we eat;
> We thank you for the birds that sing;
> We thank you for everything.

The court's rationale for its decision is expressed as follows:

> We are of the view that the verse is a prayer and that its compulsory recitation by kindergarten students in a public school comes within the proscription of the First Amendment, as interpreted by the Supreme Court in the "school prayers" cases (*Id.* at 837).

As the plaintiffs point out, if prayers which tend to teach and inculcate these virtues are not within the ambit of the ban imposed by the First Amendment against such religious activity, any religious activity of whatever nature could be justified by public officials on the basis that the activity has beneficial secular purposes; as a result the Supreme Court's admonition in *Engel* and *Schempp* would become meaningless (*Id.* at 839).

§ 2.5 Released time for religious instruction.

With the judicial restrictions to pursue religious instruction in the public schools, some school systems sought methods by which school children could receive such instruction—most notably with "released-time programs."

1. *McCollum v. Board of Education* (Ill.), 333 U.S. 203, 68 S. Ct. 461 (1948).

The basic issue in this case was whether public-school pupils could legally be released from their regular classes to attend sectarian religious instruction during the regular school in public school buildings.

The Champaign program was started by the Champaign Council on Religious Education. Although the council employed the religion teachers at no expense to the school authorities, the instructors were subject to the approval and supervision of the superintendent of schools. Moreover, classes were conducted in the regular classrooms of the school building. Students who did not choose to take the religious instruction were not released from public school duties. Reports of the presence or absence of students released from secular study for the religious instruction were made to their secular teachers.

Vashti McCollum, an avowed atheist, was opposed to the arrangement, and accordingly, began mandamus action against the Board of Education. She charged that the joint public-school religious-group program violated the First and Fourteenth Amendment to the United States Constitution. The Circuit Court dismissed her petition, and the dismissal was affirmed by the State Supreme Court, from whence it was appealed to the United States Supreme Court.

The High Court reversed the actions of the lower courts, and ruled that religious instruction in the public-school buildings during public-school time as practiced in the Champaign Public Schools, was illegal under the First and Fourteenth Amendments because it amounted to an "establishment of religion."

Justice Black, who delivered this opinion of the court stated, in part:

> The foregoing facts, without reference to others that appear in the record, show the case of tax-supported property for religious instruction and the close cooperation between the school authorities and the religious council in promoting religious education. The operation of the State's compulsory education system thus assists and is integrated with the program of religious instruction carried on by separate religious sects. Pupils compelled by law to go to school for secular education are released in part from their legal duty upon the

condition that they attend the religious classes. This is beyond all question a utilization of the tax-established and tax-supported public school system to aid religious groups to spread their faith. And it falls squarely under the ban of the First Amendment (333 U.S. 203, at 209-10).

Justice Frankfurter, in a concurring opinion, placed stress upon the "separation of State and Church" and concluded by stating:

...We find that the basic Constitutional principle of absolute Separation was violated when the State of Illinois, speaking through its Supreme Court, sustained the school authorities of Champaign in sponsoring and effectively furthering religious beliefs by its educational arrangement.

Separation means separation, not something less. Jefferson's metaphor in describing the relation between Church and State speaks of a "wall of separation" not a fine line easily overstepped. The public school is at once the symbol of our democracy and the most pervasive means for promoting our common destiny. In no activity of the State is it more vital to keep out divisive forces than in its schools, to avoid confusing, not to say fusing, what the Constitution sought to keep strictly apart... (*Id.* at 231).

Justice Reed, the lone dissenter to the court's opinion, indicated his opposition with a nineteen-page report. An excerpt of the report follows:

This Court cannot be too cautious in upsetting practices imbedded in our society by many years of experience. A state is entitled to have great leeway in its legislation when dealing with the important social problems of our population. A definite violation of legislative limits must be established. The Constitution should not be stretched to forbid natural customs in the way Courts act. ... Devotion to the great principle of religious liberty should not lead us into a rigid interpretation of the constitutional guarantee that conflicts with accepted habits of our people. This is an instance where, for me, the history of past practices is determinative of the meaning of a constitutional claim, not a decorous introduction to the study of its text (*Id.* at 256).

2. *Zorach v. Clauson* (N.Y.), 343 U.S. 306, 72 S. Ct. 679 (1952).

This case involved the same issue of a "released time program" as in the preceding case, *but under different circumstances*; the main difference being that the sectarian religious instruction would be conducted *away from* public school buildings.

This case (*Zorach*) was also carried to the United States Supreme Court, where it was held in a six to three decision that the New York law *was not unconstitutional.*

Justice Douglas, who delivered the majority opinion, stated, in part:

It takes obtuse reasoning to inject any issue of the "free exercise" of religion into the present case. No one is forced to go to the religious classroom and no religious exercise or instruction is brought to the classroom of the public schools. A student need not take religious instruction. He is left to his own desires as to the manner or time of his religious devotions, if any.

There is a suggestion that the system involves the use of coercion to get public school students into religious classrooms. There is no evidence in the record before us that supports that conclusion. The present record indeed tells us that the school authorities are neutral in this regard and do no more than release students whose parents so request. If in fact coercion were used, if it were established that any one or more teachers were using their office to persuade or force students to take the religious instruction, a wholly different case would be presented... (343 U.S. 306, at 310-11).

... The problem, like many problems in constitutional law, is one of degree....

In the *McCollum* case the classrooms were used for religious instruction and the force of the public school was used to promote that instruction. Here, as we have said, the public schools do no more than accommodate their schedules to a program of outside religious instruction. We follow the *McCollum* case. But we cannot expand it to cover the present

released time program unless separation of
Church and State means that public institutions
can make no adjustments of their schedule to
accommodate the religious needs of the people.
We cannot read into the Bill of Rights such a
philosophy of hostility to religion (*Id.* at
314-15).

Justices Black, Frankfurter, and Jackson delivered
separate dissenting opinions. The most quoted dissent
was by Justice Jackson who concluded with the
following ridicule of the majority opinion.

The day that this country ceases to be free
for irreligion it will cease to be free for religion
—except for the sect that can win political
power. The same epithetical jurisprudence
used by the Court today to beat down those
who oppose pressuring children into some
religion can devise as good epithets tomorrow
against those who object to pressuring them
into a favored religion ... the *McCollum* case
was passed like a storm in a teapot. The wall
which the Court was professing to erect
between Church and State has become even
more warped and twisted than I expected.
Today's judgment will be more interesting to
students of psychology and of the judicial
processes than to students of constitutional
law (*Id.* at 325).

3. *State ex rel. Holt v. Thompson,* 66 W.2d 659, 225
N.W.2d 678 (1975).

Several cases pertaining to "released time" are still being adjudicated. But in virtually all instances, the decisions follow the precedent set down in *Zorach*.

In this case the Wisconsin Supreme Court upheld a statute providing for a specified time of absence, determined by the board, for religious instruction *outside the school*. Brief excerpts from the opinion are illustrative.

> In the statutorily mandated plan before us, the classes for religious instruction are to be conducted elsewhere than in the public school buildings, as it is in *Zorach*, not *McCollum*, that controls. In point of fact, the Wisconsin plan and procedure is very nearly an exact carbon copy of the New York State plan approved in *Zorach* (*Id.* at 682).
>
> So we conclude that the released time for religious instruction (Sec. 188.155, Wis. State) does not violate (1) the Establishment of Religion Clause of the First Amendment of the United States Constitution; (2) the Equal Protection Clause of the Fourteenth Amendment to the United States Constitution; or (3) the freedom of worship of district school sections of the Wisconsin Constitution (*Id.* at 689).

4. *Smith v. Smith,* 391 F. Supp. 443 (W.D. Va. 1975).

At the time of this writing, this is the last reported case involving a "released time" program. Here, a federal court upheld a program where public school students were released, with their consent and the consent of parents. The religious instruction was conducted off school premises and did not interfere with nonconsenting parents having children in school. Just a brief excerpt from the court's opinion follows:

> The plaintiffs herein challenge the Harrisonburg program on both "establishment" and "free exercise" grounds, but as in *Zorach,* this court perceives the substantial constitutional issue presented to be whether this particular program amounts to an "establishment" of religion. The court is of the opinion that plaintiff's contention that the administration of the program prohibits their free exercise of religion is simply not supported by the facts (*Id.* at 446).

Chapter 3

REGULATORY CONTROL OVER THE STUDENT

§ 3.1 Student grooming.

Normally the problem of student grooming should go no further than the classroom or the principal's office. But the control over student appearance is so vigorously protested by students and particularly the parents, that the protests frequently develop into litigation.

The courts are then burdened with the perplexing problem of determining the limits of unusual styles in accordance with the best interests of the school. The problem becomes particularly difficult to resolve because what may have been considered as a reasonable risk several decades ago might not be so regarded at the present time. Consequently broad regulations governing student grooming must conform to times in which we live in order to be adjudged as reasonable. Certain modes of student grooming which are considered to be proper and sensible today might have been outlawed years ago as being improper and indecent. Several cases cited below confirm this contention.

73

1. *Leonard v. School Committee of Attleboro*, 349 Mass. 704, 212 N.E.2d 468 (1965).

This case illustrates how a boy's hairstyle considered extreme years ago could be considered normal a decade later. Here the plaintiff parents had contended that a "regulation which bars a student from attending classes solely because of length or appearance of hair is unreasonable and arbitrary." They further contended that "the challenged ruling is an invasion of family privacy touching matters occurring while he is at home and within the exclusive control of the parents."

Nevertheless the Massachusetts Supreme Court agreed with the school authorities that the boy's hair, grown well over his ears "could disrupt and impede school decorum," and therefore ruled that the school officials had the right to order him to get a normal haircut. The concluding statement of the court follows:

> So here, the domain of family privacy must give way in so far as a regulation reasonably calculated to maintain school discipline may affect it. The right of other students, and the interest of teachers, administrators, and the community at large in a well run and efficient school system are paramount.... It may be conceded that the length and appearance of the plaintiff's hair are essential to his image as a performer, and hence to his ability to follow his chosen profession. But the discretionary powers of the committee are broad, and the courts will not reverse its decision unless it can be shown it acted arbitrarily or capriciously (*Id.* at 473).

2. *Ferrell v. Dallas Independent School District* (Tex.), 261 F. Supp. 545 (1966).

A year after the *Leonard* case, a federal court was called upon to rule upon a somewhat similar issue. Here again the court upheld the action of school authorities to regulate hairstyles for boys. The court's rationale for its decision is portrayed in its concluding comment:

> Plaintiffs contend naturally that their primary interest is to get an education, but it appears that they want their education on their own terms. It is inconceivable that a school administrator could operate his school successfully if required by the courts to follow the dictates of the students as to what their appearance shall be.... Since the school authorities, by legislative grant, control the public educational system, their regulations play a part in the educational process.... It does not appear from the facts of this particular case that there has been any abuse of discretion on the part of school authorities. On the contrary, it appears that they acted reasonably under the circumstances, taking into consideration those individual students and the need for an academic atmosphere (*Id.* at 552).

3. *Griffin v. Tatum* (Ala.), 300 F. Supp. 60 (1969).

By 1970, judicial sanction for a school board's authority to regulate hairstyles for boys began to wane. This case is illustrative, where a high school boy was suspended for failure to comply with a board regulation concerning hairstyling.

75

In defending their action the school authorities offered a number of ludicrous arguments which did not convince the court, as indicated by its following declaration:

> The school authorities' "justification" as the reasons they advance for the necessity for such haircut rule, completely fail. If combing hair or passing combs in classes is distracting, the teachers, in the exercise of their authority, may stop this without requiring that the head be shorn. If there is congestion at the girls' mirrors, or if the boys are late for classes because they linger in the restrooms grooming their hair, appropriate disciplinary measures may be taken to stop this without requiring a particular hair style.... As to the fear that some students might take action against the students who wear hair longer than the regulation now permits, suffice it to say that the exercise of a constitutional right cannot be curtailed because of an undifferentiated fear that the exercise of that right will produce a violent reaction on the part of those who would deprive one of the exercise of that constitutional right (*Id.* at 63).

> In short, the freedom here protected is the right to some breathing space for the individual into which the government may not intrude without carrying a substantial burden of justification (*Id.* at 62).

4. *Gere v. Stanley* (Pa.), 320 F. Supp. 852 (1970).

Hairstyles has been a constant subject of litigation in the federal courts—almost to the state of boredom. Despite their reluctance to do so, however, they feel obligated to deal with the issue when constitutional violations are alleged. As one judge states:

> Initially it must be pointed out that it is the Court's responsibility to determine the constitutionality of this School Regulation and not the wisdom of it. I mention this because I feel the issue of hair length is receiving more attention and creating more problems than it deserves. ... But, in any event, it has become a major problem between school authorities and students, as evidenced by the deluge of court cases in the past three years and is entitled to a constitutional construction (*Id.* at 852).

5. *Graber v. Kniola*, 52 Mich. App. 269, 216 N.W.2d 925 (1974).

This case grew out of an action by students challenging the validity of a provision of the school dress code which stipulated the required length of hair for male students.

A current court upheld the validity of the provision, whereupon the students appealed. The Court of Appeals of Michigan reversed the decision of the lower court. However, its reluctance to delve very deeply into the over-stressed issue is indicated by the following remarks:

> There is really very little point to an erudite and extended discussion about the right of

school authorities to prescribe reasonable regulations of personal appearance for school attendance during school hours.

Nor will it benefit bench, bar or school authorities to hold forth at length on the undoubted right of students to choose individual attire in their hair styling. Obviously, this is not to say that young ladies of varying degrees of comeliness may (Michigan weather permitting) attend classes in bikinis. Nor may male students emulate Tarzan and attend classes in loin-cloths. Mr. Justice Cardozo, of revered memory, once cogently observed, in substance, that the law is a matter of degree (*Id.* at 926).

§ 3.2 Display of insignia as a protest gesture.

1. *Tinker v. Des Moines Independent School District* (Ia.), 393 U.S. 503, 89 S. Ct. 733 (1969).

Another method of expressing student opposition to school board regulations and certain governmental activities is the display of symbolic insignia. The advantage of this technique over the wearing of long hair or beards is that it is subject to quick adaptation.

Most noteworthy of the symbolic expression cases is *Tinker*, from which hundreds of "due process" cases have evolved. Briefly the issue concerned the legality of a school board policy banning the wearing of black armbands to symbolize and publicize objections to hostilities in Vietnam.

A district court upheld the constitutionality of the school board's action in suspending the offending students for violating the policy, on the ground that it was reasonable in order to prevent disturbance of school discipline. The Court of Appeals affirmed the decision of the district court. The United States Supreme Court, however, reversed the decisions of the lower federal courts and ruled that the wearing of armbands, as done in the Des Moines situation was akin to pure speech—a constitutional right guaranteed by the First Amendment.

Justice Fortas, who delivered the majority opinion of the court, pointed out that:

> First Amendment rights, applied in light of the special characteristics of the school environment, are available to teachers and students. It can hardly be argued that either students or teachers shed their constitutional rights at the schoolhouse gate. This has been the unmistakable holding of this Court for almost fifty years (393 U.S. 503 at 506).

> In our system, state-operated schools may not be enclaves of totalitarianism. School officials do not possess absolute authority over their students. Students in school as well as out of school are "persons" under our Constitution. They are possessed of fundamental rights which the State must respect, just as they themselves must respect their obligation to the State. In our system, students may not be regarded as closed-circuit recipients of only that which the State chooses to communicate. They may not be confined to the expression of those sentiments that are officially approved.

In the absence of a specific showing as constitutionally valid reasons to regulate their speech, students are entitled to freedom of expression of their views (*Id.* at 511).

Justice Black took sharp issue with the majority opinion. In his bitter dissent he stated:

The Court's holding in this case ushers in what I deem to be an entirely new era in which the power to control pupils by the elected "officials of state supported public schools ..." in the United States is in ultimate effect transferred to the Supreme Court (*Id.* at 515).

By way of concluding his dissent, Justice Black vigorously remarked:

One does not need to be a prophet or the son of a prophet to know that after the Court's holding today some students in Iowa schools and indeed in all schools will be ready, able, and willing to defy their teachers on practically all orders. This is the more unfortunate for the schools since groups of students all over the land are already running loose, conducting break-ins, sit-ins, lie-ins, and smash-ins. . . . This case, therefore, wholly without constitutional reasons in my judgment, subjects all the public schools in the country to the whims and caprices of their loudest-mouthed, but maybe not their brightest students. I, for one, am not fully persuaded the school pupils are wise enough, even with this Court's expert help from Washington, to run the 23,390 public

school systems in over fifty states. I wish,
therefore, wholly to disclaim any purpose on
my part to hold that the Federal Constitution
compels the teachers, parents, and elected
school officials to surrender control of the
American public school system to public school
students. I dissent (*Id.* at 525-26).

2. *Hill v. Lewis* (N.C.), 323 F. Supp. 55 (1971).

Unlike *Tinker*, students in a North Carolina high
school were *not* permitted to wear armbands (which
were black, red, white and blue) to symbolize diverse
factions with respect to war and nonwar issues. In this
case at least three different antagonistic viewpoints
were represented. Moreover, the United States District
Court found evidence showing that there was:

> . . . advance advertisement of the demon-
> stration, active group participation, marching
> in the hall ways, recruitment of other students
> to join the several groups, chanting,
> belligerent and disrespectful attitude towards
> teachers, incidents of flag disrespect and
> threats of violence (*Id.* at 58).

The court concluded:

> In the balancing of First Amendment rights
> the duty of the state to operate its public school
> system for the benefit of *all* its children must
> be protected even if governmental regulations
> incidentally limit the untrammeled exercise of
> speech, symbolic or otherwise, by those who
> would impede the education of those who
> desire to learn. The interest of the State is

superior to the rights of the protestants (*Id.* at 59).

3. *Butts v. Dallas Independent School District,* 436 F.2d 728 (1971).

A United States Court of Appeals, Fifth Circuit, explained the circumstances under which a school board could legally prohibit the wearing of armbands by students in the following statement:

> ...we believe that the Supreme Court has declared a constitutional right which school authorities must nurture and protect, not extinguish, unless they find the circumstances allow them no practical alternative. As to the existence of such circumstances, they are the judges, and if within the range where reasonable minds may differ, their decisions will govern. But there must be some inquiry, and establishment of substantial fact, to buttress the determination (*Id.* at 732).

4. *Burnside v. Byars* (Miss.), 363 F.2d 744 (1966).

Somewhat comparable to the *Tinker* and *Hill* "armband cases" are several "button cases" adjudicated in federal courts. The first such case evolved from a civil rights action for an injunction against high school officials for a regulation prohibiting students from wearing "freedom buttons."

The court voided the prohibitory regulation and ruled in favor of the students—declaring:

> We wish to make it quite clear that we do not applaud any attempt to undermine the authority of the school. We support all efforts

made by the school to fashion responsible regulations for the conduct of their students and enforcement of the punishment incurred when such regulations are violated. Obedience to duly constituted authority is a valuable tool, and respect for those in authority must be instilled in our young people.

But with all of this in mind, we must also emphasize that school officials cannot ignore expressions of feelings with which they do not wish to contend. They cannot infringe on their students' rights to free and unrestricted expression as guaranteed to them under the First Amendment to the Constitution, where the exercise of such rights in the school buildings and schoolrooms do not materially and substantially interfere with the requirements of appropriate discipline in the operation of the school (*Id.* at 749).

5. *Blackwell v. Issaquena County Board of Education* (Miss.), 363 F.2d 749 (1966).

In this companion case a contrasting decision was rendered, when the court upheld the board and ruled against the protesting students. Here, however, the court found a different situation from the one in *Burnside*, where no disruption of classes or school routine was in evidence, whereas in *Blackwell*, the court found that "students conducted themselves in a disorderly manner, disrupted classroom procedure, interfered with the proper decorum and discipline of the school and disturbed other students who did not wish to participate in the wearing of the buttons" (*Id.* at 753).

Consequently the Court of Appeals refused to grant the requested preliminary injunction, declaring its rationale for doing so:

> The judgment is affirmed without prejudice to the right of the appellants to relief upon final hearing if the facts justify such relief, emphasizing as we do the importance of the right of freedom of expression and communication as protected by the First Amendment, and the fundamental requirement that school officials should be careful in their monitoring of student expressions in circumstances in which such expression does not substantially interfere with the operation of the school (*Id.* at 754).

§ 3.3 Student demonstrations.

1. *Edwards v. South Carolina,* 372 U.S. 229 (1963).

Student demonstrations are viewed as a form of expression. If conducted peacefully at the proper times and proper places they are likely to receive judicial sanction—at least in the federal courts. For example, in this case, high school students joined college students in attempting to peacefully express their dissatisfaction with allegedly present conditions of discriminatory action against Negroes.

Circumstances involved in the case are stated in certiorari to the Supreme Court of South Carolina as follows:

> Feeling aggrieved by laws of South Carolina which allegedly "prohibited Negro privileges," petitioners, 187 Negro high school and college

students, peacefully assembled at the site of the State Government and there peacefully expressed their grievances "to the citizens of South Carolina." When told by police officials that they must disperse within 15 minutes on pain of arrest, they failed to do so and sang patriotic and religious songs after one of their leaders had delivered a "religious harangue." There was no evidence of violence on their part or on the part of any member of the crowd watching them; but petitioners were arrested and convicted of the common-law crime of breach of the peace, which the State Supreme Court said is not susceptible to exact definition *(Id.* at 229).

Although the convictions of the demonstrators were affirmed by the South Carolina Supreme Court, its ruling was reversed by the United States Supreme Court. In support of its action the High Court spoke as follows:

The Fourteenth Amendment does not permit a State to make criminal the peaceful expression of unpopular views. A function of free speech under our system of government is to invite dispute. It may indeed best serve the high purpose when it induces a condition of unrest, creates dissatisfaction with conditions as they are, or even stirs people to anger. It may strike at prejudice and preconceptions and have profound unsettling effects as it presses for acceptance of an idea. That is why freedom of speech is protected against censorship or

punishment, unless shown likely to produce a
clear and present danger of a serious
substantive evil that arises far above public
inconvenience, annoyance, or unrest ... (*Id.* at
237).

2. *Tate v. Board of Education of Jonesboro, Arkansas
Special School District,* 453 F.2d 975 (U.S.C.A. 8th Cir.,
1972).

In this case twenty-nine black students participated in
a group demonstration by getting up and leaving a pep
assembly in protest to the playing of "Dixie." The
students were accordingly advised that the walkout
action was deemed disruptive to the school program so
they were being suspended.

The plaintiff students argued that "their departure
from the pep rally was symbolic action guarded from
suppression by the Free Speech Clause." They cited
Tinker to support their argument.

The court rejected the argument, pointing out that in
Tinker, the Supreme Court was dealing with "direct
privacy, First Amendment rights akin to pure speech,"
in contrast to "aggressive, disruptive action or even
group demonstration," as in the *Tate* case.

In upholding the action of the school authorities the
court concluded its opinion with the following
statement:

> On this record we cannot say that the tune
> "Dixie" constitutes a badge of slavery or that
> the playing of the tune under the facts as
> presented constituted officially sanctioned
> racial abuse. Such a ruling would lead to the
> prohibition of the playing of many of our most
> famous tunes.

... The action taken by the school authorities obviously averted serious trouble and was not only practical but clearly and properly within the rights of the school officials if we are to have any discipline in our public schools. Court intervention could in such situations only serve to fan embers of unrest. The court should never interfere except where there is a clear case of constitutional infringement (*Id.* at 982).

§ 3.4 Freedom of speech and press.

1. *Scoville v. Board of Education of Joliet Township High School District 204* (Ill.), 286 F. Supp. 988 (1968), 425 F.2d 10 (1970).

This case developed as a result of students distributing a controversial literary journal entitled "Grass High" which contained, in an editorial, derogatory statements about the school administration, such as that which follows:

> The editorial went on to criticize school attendance regulations as "utterly idiotic and asinine" and concluded that "Our whole system of education with all its arbitrary rules and schedules seems dedicated to nothing but wasting time." Elsewhere, the editorial accused the senior dean of the school of having a "sick mind" (286 F. Supp. at 989).

A United States District Court upheld the school district in the suspension of Scoville, and supported its decision with statements such as the following:

The freedom of speech and association protected by the First and Fourteenth Amendments are not "absolute" and are subject to constitutional restrictions for the protection of the social interest in government, order and morality ... the activities of high school students do not always fall within the same category as the conduct of college students, the former being in a much more adolescent and immature stage of life and less able to screen facts from propaganda.

While there is a certain aura of sacredness attached to the First Amendment, nevertheless the First Amendment rights must be balanced against the duty and obligation of the state to educate students in an orderly and decent manner to protect the rights not of a few but of all the students in the school system. The line of reason must be drawn somewhere in this area of ever expanding permissibility. Gross disrespect and contempt for the officials of an educational institution may be justification not only for suspension but also expulsion of a student (*Id.* at 242).

On appeal, however, a United States Court of Appeals *reversed* the decision of the District Court with the following concluding remarks:

the Board could not have reasonably forecast that the publication and distribution of this paper to the students would substantially disrupt or materially interfere with school procedures. ... In view of our conclusion that the complaint "on its face" discloses an unjustified invasion of plaintiff's First and Fourteenth Amendment rights, it follows that we agree with plaintiffs that the Board applied the Illinois statute in an unconstitutional manner. 425 F.2d 10, at 15 (1970).

2. *Bayer v. Kinzler,* 383 F. Supp. 1164 (E.D.N.Y. 1974).

In this case, action was taken challenging the seizure of a sex education supplement to a high school newspaper. The District Court held that the seizure of the material and refusal to allow its distribution were unconstitutional violations of the First and Fourteenth Amendment rights.

In following the reasoning in *Tinker,* the court commented as follows:

> Even assuming that the newspaper is part of the "curriculum," defendants' "intrusion" theory does not furnish a reasonable basis for interference with student speech. The invalidity of defendants' theory is demonstrated by examining the impact it would have in the factual context of *Tinker.* Social studies surely is part of the school curriculum. Under defendants' theory, the petitioners in *Tinker* might well not be permitted to wear armbands to protest the Vietnam war since their symbolic protest dealt with an area of the curriculum. Moreover, if defendants' theory is adopted, the presence of articles in the school newspaper dealing with political topics will make the newspaper subject to seizure in the

future. Such a result is inconsistent with the right of high school students to free expression, subject to well-defined and relatively narrow limitations (*Id.* at 1166).

3. *Cintron v. State Board of Education*, 384 F. Supp. 674 (D.P.R. 1974).

This case involved the suspension of a junior high school student for the distribution of handbills to other students. The handbills "called for the justification of students in a subdivision of a political party which advocates Puerto Rican independence" (*Id.* at 675).

In upholding the students' action, the court disregarded the Board's contention that the action violated school board rules and regulations. A brief excerpt of the court's opinion follows:

> These regulations are about as broad a ban upon free expression in school as can be imagined. . . .

> The school authorities contend that these rules are needed to prevent political and other agitation current in the Commonwealth from invading the schools and disrupting the educational process. This seems to us to be precisely the kind of "undifferentiated fear" which the *Tinker* Court made clear could not support infringement upon the First Amendment rights of students (*Id.* at 679).

§ 3.5 Search and seizure.

1. *In re Donaldson*, 75 Cal. Rptr. 220 (1969).

Litigation frequently occurs when school personnel search students or student lockers in the attempt to suppress the possession of harmful drugs or other incriminating objects of wrongdoing. For example, in this case a vice principal of a high school searched a student's locker where he found cigarettes made of marijuana.

A juvenile court found the student guilty of violating a section of the Health and Safety Code (possession of marijuana); on appeal, the Court of Appeals affirmed, making the following comments:

> The legislature, in recognizing the dangerous condition created on school premises by the possession thereon of drugs, enacted section 10603 of the Education Code, which provides that for the protection of other pupils in the public school, a pupil who has on school premises or elsewhere used, sold or been in possession of narcotics or other hallucinogenic drugs or substances, may be suspended or expelled (*Id.* at 222).

> The school stands *in loco parentis* and shares, in matters of school discipline, the parent's right to use moderate force to obtain obedience ... and that right extends to the search of the appellant's locker under the factual situation herein related. The marijuana was not obtained by an unlawful search and seizure (*Id.* at 223).

2. *State v. Stein,* 203 Kan. 638, 456 P.2d 1. (1969).

This case indicates that a student's right of privacy is not violated when "his" locker is searched. Although Stein contended that the evidence found in the locker was inadmissible because he had not been given a *Miranda* warning prior to the search, the Kansas Supreme Court ruled otherwise and in so doing gave emphasis to the peculiar legal nature of a student's locker:

> Although a student may have control of his school locker as against fellow students, his possession is not exclusive against the school and its officials. A school does not supply its students with lockers for illicit use in harboring pilfered property or harmful substances. We deem it a proper function of school authorities to inspect the lockers under their control and to prevent their use in illicit ways or for illegal purposes. We believe this right of inspection is inherent in the authority vested in school administration and that the same must be retained and exercised in the management of our schools if their educational functions are to be maintained and the welfare of the student bodies preserved (*Id.* at 3).

3. *People v. Scott D.,* 34 N.Y.2d 483 (1974).

While school authorities may have the right to search students' lockers, that authority may not extend to the search of the student himself, especially in a forced state of undress.

In this case it was revealed that a student had been under observation by a teacher on suspicion that he carried drugs on his person. Consequently, a security coordinator informed the principal of the student's "unusual behavior" and was instructed to bring him to the principal's office. "There in the presence of a boys' dean and the principal, defendant was searched by the security coordinator, and after discovery in his wallet of thirteen glassine envelopes containing a white powder, made to strip" (*Id.* at 486).

The court held that the search exceeded bounds of reasonableness and concluded with the following statement:

> The issue may not be left without emphasizing that although the necessities for a public school search may be greater than for one outside the school, the psychological damage that would be risked on sensitive children by random search insufficiently justified by the necessities is not tolerable. And it must also be emphasized that the scope of undue risk of psychological harm, will vary significantly with the age and mental development of the child (*Id.* at 490).

4. *"J. W.," by his guardian v. Board of Education of the Town of Hammonton, et al.* (Dec. of N.J. Comm. of Educ. Nov. 25, 1975).

This case is typical of several on which the Commissioner has had to rule in recent years. Here, a tenth-grade pupil, referred to as "J. W." in the report, was expelled from school on June 12, 1975 until January 8, 1976, for possession and consumption of marijuana on school property.

Guardians of "J. W." alleged that the imposed expulsion was "improperly severe and constitutionally defective." However, the Commissioner ruled otherwise. He stated, in part:

> The possession and use of illicit drugs by pupils in our public schools must be dealt with swiftly in order to prevent their introduction to other pupils particularly those of younger years (*Id.* at 12).

> The Commissioner is constrained to repeat that the possession or use by pupils in a schoolhouse or on school grounds of marijuana or any other controlled dangerous substance described in the law may not be condoned. It is the considered judgment of the Commissioner that to leave such conduct unpunished would only create a school atmosphere which would encourage younger pupils and more pupils to experiment with controlled dangerous substances. Local boards of education must deal with such problems in a manner which will discourage violations of the law (*Id.* at 15-16).

5. *State v. Young,* 234 Ga. 488, 216 S.E.2d 586 (Sup. Ct. of Ga. 1975).

In this case the Supreme Court of Georgia reversed a decision of the Court of Appeals which had convicted a high school student of the misdemeanor of possession of marijuana.

> The search in question was made after the assistant principal observed Young, a seventeen-year-old student, on the premises of

the public school he attended. Young was with two other students during school hours and as the principal approached "one of the fellows jumped up and put something down, ran his hand in his pants." The three students were then directed to empty their pockets and Young produced marijuana (*Id.* at 588).

In defense of the assistant principal's action, the Supreme Court stated:

> ... It is not necessary to decide what good faith conduct by a searching teacher or official would fail to meet that standard, because the student's acts in the case before us, involving a furtive gesture and an obvious consciousness of guilt by these students at the approach of the assistant principal, clearly gave him adequate reason for the searches he made. The search of Young was entirely proper under the Fourth Amendment. Young has suffered no abridgment of his Fourth Amendment right to be free from *unreasonable* searches and seizures. The search made here was reasonable under the standard we announce today (*Id.* at 593).

In a *dissenting opinion*, Justice Gunter declared:

> My view, of course, is that there must be "probable cause" for a search of a student in a public school by a school official, and such a search without "probable cause" violates the Fourth Amendment rights of a student as a citizen. A student, in my view, cannot be

stripped of his Fourth Amendment rights at the entrance to the public school. Nor do I think that the Fourth Amendment rights of a high school student are a diluted version of the Fourth Amendment rights of an adult (*Id.* at 599).

§ 3.6 Limits of control off school grounds.

1. *Hobbs v. Germany*, 94 Miss. 469, 49 So. 515 (1909).

This early precedential case is still frequently cited in school-law writings because of its present-day relevance. It established the legal principle denoting the legal boundaries of parental versus school control over the pupil off school grounds and after school hours.

It evolved from a school requirement that all pupils must stay in their homes and study from 7 to 9 p.m. One evening, during the designated home-study period, a sixteen-year-old boy was apprehended attending a religious service with his father, whereupon school authorities attempted to exact punishment by expulsion from school for violation of the rule.

The father filed suit, alleging that "the adoption of the rule is beyond the lawful power of either the trustees or the teachers and constitutes a usurpation of authority not conferred upon them by law." The Supreme Court of Mississippi agreed with the allegation as indicated by the following statement:

> Certainly a rule of the school, which invades the home and wrests from the parent his right to control his child around his own hearthstone, is inconsistent with any law that has governed the parent in this state, and the

writer of this opinion does hope that it will be inconsistent with any law that will ever operate here so long as liberty lasts, and children are taught to revere and look to their parents. In the home the parental authority is and should be supreme, and it is a misguided zeal that attempts to wrest it from them. . . . While in the teacher's charge, the parent would have no right to invade the schoolroom and interfere with him in its management. On the other hand, when the pupil is released, and sent back to its home, neither the teachers nor directors have the authority to follow him thither, and govern his conduct while under the parental age (*Id.* at 517).

2. *O'Rourke v. Walker*, 102 Conn. 130, 128 A. 25 (1925).

There may sometimes be certain circumstances in which a teacher or principal may have, not only the authority but also the responsibility, to exercise control over pupils away from and after school hours. For example, in the instant case, an assault action was brought against a school principal who punished a boy for abusing small girl pupils on their way home from school. Even though the incident took place after the boy had reached home, the court sustained a judgment in favor of the principal, and said:

Examination of the authorities clearly reveals the true test of the teacher's right and jurisdiction to punish for offenses not committed on the school property or going and returning therefrom, but after the return of the pupil to the parental abode, to be not the time or place of the offense, but its effect upon the morale and efficiency of the school, whether it in fact is detrimental to its good order, and to the welfare and advancement of the pupils therein ... (*Id.* at 26).

To the plaintiff's argument that "the proper resort to correct such an abuse is the parents of such offenders, or public prosecutors," the court replied:

Some parents would dismiss the matter by saying that they could give no attention to children's quarrels; many would even champion their children as being all right in their conduct. The public authorities would very properly say, unless the offense resulted in quite serious injury, that such affrays were too trifling to deserve their attention. Yet the harm to the school has been done, and its proper conduct and operation seriously harmed, by such acts. Correction will usually be sought in vain at the hands of the parents; it can only be successfully applied by the teachers (*Id.* at 27).

§ 3.7 Restraining affiliation with secret societies.

School patrons have questioned the authority of legislatures to enact anti-fraternity statutes, as well as school boards to impose restrictions and penalties on those who affiliate with the secret societies. As evidenced by the number of court cases, the controversy has been so severe as to often lead to litigation.

Of the score of cases dealing with the issue, only *one* (*Wright v. Board of Education of St. Louis,* 295 Mo. 466, 246 S.W. 43 (Sup. Ct. 1922)), reported by a court of record, was an anti-fraternity rule declared illegal. In all the other cases the courts have upheld the anti-fraternity regulations. Because of similarity in the cases only a few will be referred to here.

1. *Holroyd v. Eibling,* 116 Ohio App. 440, 188 N.E.2d 797 (1962).

This is a typical anti-fraternity case, growing out of a Columbus School Board regulation which "prohibited any pupil holding membership in a fraternity or sorority from participating in . . . any athletic, literary, military, musical, dramatic, service, scientific, scholastic, and other similar activities of his school including honor societies, or honor organizations . . ." (*Id.* at 799).

Plaintiff parents objected to the regulations on the grounds that if enforced, the school authorities would gain complete control of the pupils' activities and thus deny parents their responsibility to select associates for their children away from school and after school hours. The court was not impressed by this argument and, with the support of a precedent established by previous decisions on the issue, the Court of Appeals of Ohio stated:

> The rationale of these decisions is that a board of education is vested with broad discretionary powers in adopting a policy prohibiting affiliation with such organizations in the government, management and discipline of the schools, that such regulations do not deprive the pupils or parents of any *natural* or

constitutional rights or privileges; that, when, in the opinion of the school authorities, such organizations have a deleterious influence and are found to be inimical to the best interests of the school, a school board is authorized, even in the absence of a specific statute granting such power, to adopt regulations prohibiting them; and that such power is inherent in a board of education (*Id.* at 801).

2. *Passel v. Fort Worth Independent School District,* 429 S.W.2d 917 (Ct. of Civ. App. Texas 1968).

Throughout the proceedings in this case, the Court of Civil Appeals of Texas did not express much concern about several grievances of the plaintiff parents, with the exception of one claiming that "the school board requirement was an invasion of the right of parents to control their children." The court expressed its rejection of this argument in the following terms:

The argument advanced by the appellants which causes us the most concern is that the statute involved constitutes an invasion of the right of parental control over their children. Certainly neither the school system [n]or the church or any other organization however well motivated should or could replace parents in the rearing of a child. We would not wish to say anything in this opinion which would weaken this basic and fundamental right. But we do not believe that requiring parents to sign the Supplemental Enrollment Form constitutes an invasion of parental control as to render it constitutionally invalid. We believe that our duly constituted independent school districts with appropriate guidance from the Legislature should run our public school system. While the last thing we would wish to do is to interfere with the right of freedom of association or the civil rights of the students involved, we must maintain an orderly system of administration of our public schools (*Id.* at 925).

3. *Robinson v. Sacramento City Unified School District*, 245 Cal. App. 2d 278, 53 Cal. Rptr. 781 (1966).

Litigation involving the legality of secret societies in the public schools is not limited to fraternities. For example, a case was adjudicated in a California court where a member of a girls' club, called the "Manana Club" sought to have a rule of the school board declared invalid which prohibited a fraternity, sorority or *club* in which membership was determined secretly.

Although the court admittedly saw some merits in a secret society, such as the "Manana Club," it left it to the judgment of the school board to determine if the alleged merits were sufficient enough to justify existence of the club. In holding the school board rule *valid*, the court declared:

High school fraternities, sororities and clubs undoubtedly accomplish good, mostly to those who belong to them, giving them a sense of security, a feeling of being wanted. But the school board has said the harm these societies do outweighs the good, that they are "inimical" to the "government, discipline and morale of the pupils." School boards are

professionals in this field, the courts are
laymen; the boards are close to the day-to-day
affairs of the pupils of secondary schools and
the problems which arise in a school
community, courts are removed therefrom (*Id.*
at 789).

Here the school board is not dealing with adults
but with adolescents in their formative years. And
it is not dealing with activities which occur only
within the home and which, therefore, might be
said to relate exclusively to parental jurisdiction
and control. It is dealing with express statutory
mandate with activities which reach into the school
and which reasonably may be said to interfere with
the educational process, with the morale of
high-school student bodies as a whole and which
also may reasonably be said not to foster
democracy (as the Manana Club by its admitted
activities practices) (*Id.* at 790).

§ 3.8 Barring married students from non-classroom activities.

The concern of school officials over student
marriages is reflected in the numerous policies
formulated to regulate school activities of married
students as a means of curbing high-school marriages.
Some of the board regulations have been so controversial and objectionable as to trigger litigation.

1. *Kissick v. Garland Independent School District,*
330 S.W.2d 708 (Ct. of Civ. App. of Texas 1959).
This is the first applicable case dealing with the issue.
Kissick, a football player, sought to restrain
enforcement of a board resolution providing that:

married students or previously married
students be restricted wholly to classroom
work, that they be barred from participating in
athletics or other exhibitions, and that they not
be permitted to hold class offices or other
positions of honor (*Id.* at 709).

The Texas court upheld the board's policy despite
Kissick's argument that the resolution was arbitrary,
capricious, discriminatory, and unreasonable, and was
violative of public policy in that it penalized marriage.
Apparently the court placed considerable weight upon
findings of a PTA study indicating "ill effect of married
students participating in extra-curricular activities with
unmarried students" (*Id.* at 710).

That the court's decision was not exactly based upon
the merits of the board's resolution is reflected in the
following passage:

> Boards of Education, rather than the Courts,
> are charged with the important and difficult
> duty of operating the public schools. So, it is
> not a question of whether this or that
> individual judge or court considers a given
> regulation adopted by the Board as expedient.
> The Court's duty, regardless of its personal
> views, is to uphold the Board's regulation
> unless it is generally viewed as being arbitrary
> and unreasonable. Any other policy would
> result in confusion detrimental to the progress
> and efficiency of our public school system
> (*Id.* at 712).

2. *Holt v. Shelton,* 341 F. Supp. 821 (U.S.D.C. M.D. Tenn. 1972).

Several cases during the sixties indicated the precedent established in *Kissick* was beginning to erode. A rash of cases in the early 1970's bears out this contention. The instant case is illustrative in which a *girl* student was involved.

The girl successfully sought an injunction prohibiting school officials from prohibiting her, because she was married, from participating in activities and functions other than those for which credit for graduation was given. The court's rationale in support of the girl is forcefully stated as follows:

In the case at bar, the regulation which plaintiff is challenging infringes upon her fundamental right to marry by severely limiting her right to an education. The defendants have failed utterly to show that the infringement upon either of these two rights promotes a "compelling" state interest. Indeed, they have failed to show that the regulation in question is even rationally related to—not to mention "necessary" to promote in *any* legitimate state interest at all. Instead it is apparent that the sole purpose and effect of the regulation is to discourage, by actually punishing, marriages which are perfectly legal under the laws of Tennessee and which are thus fully consonant with the public policy of the State. It is the opinion of the court that such a regulation is repugnant to the Constitution of the United States in that it impermissibly infringes upon the due process and equal protection of the law of those students who come within its ambit (*Id.* at 823).

3. *Moran v. School District #7, Yellowstone County,* 350 F. Supp. 1180 (U.S.D.C.D. Montana 1972).

Also in this case a preliminary injunction was granted to a married student who was held by the board to be ineligible to play varsity football because "presence of married students in extracurricular activities would result in reasonable likelihood of moral pollution." Since no factual evidence to this charge could be produced, the court stated:

> Montana Supreme Court has recognized the importance of extracurricular activities as an integral part of the total education process. Courts have begun to recognize that extracurricular activities such as football are "generally recognized as a fundamental ingredient of the educational process" (*Id.* at 1184).

> Since there is no authority expressly granted to the board to regulate marriages and since there is clear public policy with regard to marriage then to constitute a valid exercise of state law the school board's authority to discriminate on the basis of marriage must first be found in its expressed function of providing education and then balanced against the interest which it may violate (*Id.* at 1185).

4. *Hollon v. Mathis Independent School District*, 358 F. Supp. 1269 (U.S.D.C. S.W. Tex. 1973).

This is another case in which a temporary injunction was granted against enforcement of a school district policy prohibiting married students from engaging in interscholastic league athletic activities.

The married student involved was a senior in high school. He had been active in athletics, lettering in both football and basketball. He was considered to be a good athlete, was in line for a college scholarship and intended to continue his education at the college level.

Nonetheless, because of his marriage, he was barred from participating in the athletic contests. The school officials attempted to justify their policy by referring to the "alarming number of marriages and drop-outs."

The court responded to the board's action as follows:

> The Superintendent and the members of the School Board are certainly to be commended on a consistent effort to meet these most serious problems attendant with the high rate of high school drop-outs. However, the court has decided there is no justifiable relationship between the marriage of high school athletes and the overall drop-out problem, nor does it appear that preventing a good athlete, although married, from continuing to play in whatever game he may excel, would in any way deter other marriages or otherwise enhance the drop-out problem (*Id.* at 1271).

5. *Bell v. Lone Oak Independent School District*, 507 S.W.2d 636 (Tex. 1974).

In this case a student was successful in having enjoined the enforcement of a school regulation designed to prohibit married students from participating in extracurricular activities. A portion of the litigated regulation stipulated that:

> The married student cannot be elected to an office, or if already elected, must resign . . . cannot participate in athletics, pep squad, class plays, social events such as junior-senior banquet, football banquet, etc. (*Id.* at 637).

Although the court expressed reluctance to deal with this much-litigated issue again, it did so, and ruled decisively in favor of the student. In doing so, the court declared:

> The quoted rule of the Lone Oak Independent School District sets up a classification of individuals to be treated differently from the remainder of the school students without being designed to promote a compelling state interest. . . . The burden of proof is upon the school district to show that its rule should be upheld as a necessary restraint to promote a compelling state interest.
>
> It is the public policy of this state to encourage marriage rather than living together unmarried. To promote that public policy, we have sanctioned by statute the marriage ceremony and through the years have jealously guarded the bonds of matrimony. It therefore seems illogical to say that a school district can make a rule punishing a student for

entering into a status authorized and sanctioned by the laws of this state. We find no logical bases for such rule. We are not unmindful of the decision in *Kissick* . . . involving a situation similar to the one in this case. There the court held that it was not arbitrary, capricious, discriminatory or unreasonable to bar married students from participating in athletics or other extracurricular activities. Our holding in this case is in direct opposition to *Kissick*.

We have chosen not to follow *Kissick* because we feel that the rule there should be abandoned for one that is nondiscriminatory and which does not violate constitutionally guaranteed rights . . . (*Id.* at 638).

˙ 6. *Indiana High School Athletic Association v. Raike,* 329 N.E.2d 66 (Ind. Ct. App. 1975).

In this recent case, a school district and an athletic association were *unsuccessful* in their appeal from a permanent injunction preventing them from prohibiting married high school students from participating in athletics and other extracurricular programs.

The litigated rule of the school district stipulated that: "Married students, or those who have been married, are in school chiefly to meet academic needs and they will be disqualified from participating in extracurricular activities and Senior activities except Commencement and Baccalaureate" (*Id.* at 69-70).

The rule of the athletic association supplemented the school rule as follows: "Students who are or have been married are not eligible for participating in intra-school athletic competition" (*Id.* at 70).

Testimony by school personnel and consultants who attempted to justify the existence of the above rules is summarized as follows:

1. Married students need time to discharge economic and family responsibilities, and participating in athletics and extracurricular activities would interfere with these responsibilities.

2. Teenage marriages should be discouraged so as to reduce the high percentage of divorce and school drop-out rates among married students.

3. Athletes serve as models or heroes to other students and teenage marriages are usually the result of pregnancy so that immorality is encouraged if married students participate without sanction in athletics.

4. If married students participate in athletics, a double standard must be applied, thereby causing discipline, training and administrative problems.

5. Unwholesome interaction between married and non-married students is prevented by avoidance of undesirable "locker room talk" (*Id.* at 70).

In disregarding these arguments, the Indiana Court of Appeals, Second District, rendered the following concise decision:

It is our opinion that the Rules prohibiting a married high school student from participating in athletics and extracurricular activities do not bear a fair and substantial relation to the objective sought, and therefore deny Raike equal protection of the laws contrary to the Fourteenth Amendment of the U.S. Constitution (*Id.* at 71).

§ 3.9. Sex discrimination in sports.

It is generally agreed that one of the most glaring examples of sex discrimination is that which operates against female students who wish to participate in competitive sports. However, that situation has come to an abrupt halt by virtue of Title IX of the Education Amendments of 1972, the pertinent section of which provides:

> No person in the United States shall, on the basis of sex, be excluded from participation in, be denied the benefits of, or be subjected to discrimination under any education program or activity receiving Federal financial assistance.

As a result of this federal legislation, numerous court cases have arisen in which school systems have failed to comply with *equal* educational opportunities — particularly in competitive sports.

1. *Brenden v. Independent School District # 742*, 342 F. Supp. 1224 (Minn. 1972).

The facts of this case indicate that two girls who desired to participate in certain sports offered at their respective schools were denied the right to do so.

Peggy Brenden, an eighteen-year-old senior, desired to become a member of the boys' tennis team at her school. She was considered "an excellent tennis player." The tennis program open to girls was inadequate to meet her aspiration.

The other girl, Tony St. Pierre, a seventeen-year-old junior, desired to become a member of the boys' cross-country and cross-country skiing teams at her school. She was considered an "excellent young athlete."

Both girls were informed that they could not participate in the boys' teams "because of a rule of the Minnesota High School League preventing participation by girls on boys' interscholastic athletic teams" (*Id.* at 1227).

The girls won their suit as indicated by the following statement of the court:

> In summary, the court is confronted with a situation where two high school girls wish to take part in certain interscholastic boys' athletics. . . . Brought to its base, then Peggy Brenden and Tony St. Pierre are being prevented from participating . . . solely on the basis of the fact of sex and sex alone. The court is thus of the opinion that in these factual circumstances, the application of the League rule to Peggy Brenden and Tony St. Pierre is arbitrary and unreasonable, in violation of the equal protection clause of the Fourteenth Amendment. For this reason, the application of the rule to these two girls cannot stand . . . (*Id.* at 1234).

2. *Gilpin v. Kansas State High School Activities Association, Inc.,* 377 F. Supp. 1233 (Kan. 1974).

Here again "a civil rights suit was brought by a female high school student who claimed deprivation of equal protection due to state high school activities association's rule which claimed to have prevented plaintiff from participating in cross-country competition solely on the basis of sex" (*Id.* at 1233).

The court upheld the girl's contention with the following declaration:

> . . . the practical effect of the Association's rule prohibiting mixed competition is not merely to prevent Tammie Gilpin's participation on a boys' cross-country team, but rather to completely bar her from participating in cross-country competition. Rather than contributing to the advancement of girls' interscholastic competition, the rule acts to totally deprive Tammie Gilpin of the opportunity to compete at all, solely on the basis of her sex. Thus, although the Association's overall objective is commendable and legitimate, the method employed to accomplish that objective is simply over-broad in its reach. It is precisely this sort of overinclusiveness which the Equal Protection Clause disdains. . . . Accordingly, it is ordered that Tammie Gilpin be permitted to compete on the boys' cross-country team . . . (*Id.* at 1243).

3. *National Organization for Women, Essex County Chapter v. Little League Baseball, Inc.,* 127 N.J. Super. 522, 318 A.2d 33 (1974).

This case developed from a complaint of violation of the New Jersey Law Against Discrimination — and particularly against the provision prohibiting girls from playing baseball in the "Little League."

The defense by "Little League," in essence, was that because of physical differences between the sexes, girls as a class, were more prone to injury than were boys when playing with a hard ball.

After considerable evidence was produced on both sides of the issue, the hearing officers held that:

> Little League had not borne its burden of establishing that girls of 8 to 12 are so physiologically inferior to boys of the same age group as to preclude them as a class from competing as safely and successfully as boys in the game (*Id.* at 35).

Relying on the findings produced, the court upheld the order to "admit girls from 8 to 12 to participation in their baseball program conducted in the State."

With respect to both the physiological and psychological aspects of the issue the court stated:

> We conclude there was substantial credible evidence in the record to permit the Division to find as a fact that girls of ages 8-12 are not as a class subject to a materially greater hazard of injury while playing baseball than boys of that age group. . . . Thus the factor of safety does not militate for a determination that the nature of Little League baseball reasonably restricts participation in it at the 8-12 age level to boys. We regard the psychological testimony on both sides as too speculative to rest any fact-finding on it . . . (*Id.* at 36-37).

Chapter 4

STUDENT DISCIPLINARY PRACTICES

§ 4.1 Application of the in loco parentis doctrine.

Legally, the teacher possesses limited discretionary authority in disciplining students. The authority transcends from the common-law doctrine referred to as *in loco parentis*, which, when translated means "in place of the parent." The classic phrase may be traced to Blackstone's *Commentaries*:

> A parent may also delegate part of his parental authority, during his life, to the tutor or schoolmaster of his child; who is then *in loco parentis*, and has such a portion of the power of the parent, viz. that the restraint and correction, as may be necessary to answer the purpose for which he is employed (Blackstone, *Commentaries of the Laws of England* 453, T. Cooley, ed., 1884).

Attention should be given to the last words of the Blackstone phrase *as may be necessary to answer the purposes for which he is employed.* Obviously, it is not implied that the doctrine authorizes school authorities to *completely* displace parental authority in all matters relating to the school. Disregard for the limitation is cause for much of the litigation on the issue.

1. *Woodman v. Litchfield Community School District No. 12,* 242 N.E.2d 780 (Ill. App. 1968).

The limited scope of the *in loco parentis* principle is frequently violated by broadening the scope of the teacher's authority and responsibility beyond that of maintaining discipline. A statutory provision in the Illinois laws is illustrative:

> Teachers . . . shall maintain discipline in the schools. In all matters relating to the discipline in and conduct of the schools and the school children, they stand in the relation of parents and guardians to the pupils. This relationship shall extend to all activities connected with the school program and may be exercised at any time for the safety and supervision of the pupils in the absence of their parents or guardians (*Id.* at 782).

In upholding the validity of the statute, the Appellate Court of Illinois, Fifth District, stated:

> The statutory enactment would protect a teacher from liability for mere negligence in supervising or maintaining discipline because of the status conferred; that of a parent or guardian in relation to all the pupils in the classroom. No liability would attach to a parent or one having the relation of parent absent an event constituting willful or wanton conduct (*Id.* at 782).

2. *Morris v. Ortiz,* 103 Ariz. 119, 437 P.2d 652 (1968).

116

A more prevalent line of reasoning is expressed by a dissenting judge on the Supreme Court of Arizona in a teacher liability case:

> The relationship of a public school teacher to his pupil is in some respects in loco parentis. Having the right to control and supervise the pupil, there is a correlative duty to act as a reasonable and prudent parent would in like circumstances. . . . The rationale of in loco parentis does not however apply in determining liability for a negligent tort against the pupil. In most jurisdictions the parent is not liable for negligent tort against his child, but the public school teacher may be (*Id.* at 657).

3. *Guerrieri v. Tyson*, 147 Pa. Super. 239, 24 A.2d 468 (1942).

The limited authority of a teacher over the student in matters "necessary to answer the purposes for which he is employed" is exemplified in this early Pennsylvania case, where a teacher attempted to treat a student's infected finger by immersing it in scalding water against his will, which aggravated the infection, and permanently disfigured his hand.

The court agreed to the delegated parental authority implied from the relationship of teacher and pupils, but in ruling against the teacher in the instant case, the court stated:

> . . . a teacher may inflict reasonable corporal punishment on a pupil to enforce discipline . . . but there is no implied delegation of

117

authority to exercise her lay judgment, as a
parent may, in the matter of the treatment of
injury or disease suffered by a pupil . . . (*Id.* at
469).

4. *Duda v. Gaines*, 12 N.J. Super. 326, 79 A.2d 695
(1951).

This case refers to alleged negligence of a teacher,
standing *in loco parentis*, who failed to obtain medical
assistance for a school pupil who was injured during
football practice.

In rendering judgment for the defendant teacher, the
court ruled there was insufficient proof to indicate the
existence of the alleged emergency, and accordingly
made the following statement:

> The emergency from which would arise the
> stipulated legal duty can be said to exist when
> a reasonable man having the knowledge of
> facts known to the teacher or which they might
> reasonably be expected to know would
> recognize a pressing necessity for medical aid,
> and the dictates of humanity, duty and fair
> dealing would require that there be put in the
> boy's reach such medical care and other
> assistance as the situation might in reason
> demand so that the pupil might be relieved of
> his hurt and more serious consequences be
> avoided (*Id.* at 696).

5. *Chilton v. Cook County School District No. 207,
Maine Township*, 26 Ill. App. 3d 459, 325 N.E.2d 666
(1975).

A school's authority to determine the curricular activities in which a student must participate, by virtue of *in loco parentis* was voided by an Illinois court in 1975.

Here a school district was held liable for damages sustained by a fifteen-year-old freshman who was severely injured in an unsuccessful attempt to comply with a curricular requirement that "the trampoline course was required of all freshmen students without regard to any demonstrated ability or experience on the trampoline" (*Id.* at 668).

The defendant school district argued that the School Code conveys broad discretionary authority to educators who "stand in relation of parents and guardians to the pupil" and that "this relationship shall extend to all activities with the school program and may be exercised at any time" (*Id.* at 669).

> In refuting this argument, the court stated:
> . . . we note that the trial court refused to instruct the jury that the *in loco parentis* standard was applicable to the case at bar and that the trial court declared that the basis for its ruling on the point was its belief that Section 24-24 applied only to disciplinary situations. We agree, and we find that the cited section does not specifically outline a broader basis for a school's disciplinary and supervisory powers and does not make such broader basis a matter of state law (*Id.* at 671).

§ 4.2 Due process rights of students.

The legal term "due process" stems from the Fifth and Fourteenth Amendments to the United States Constitution.

The Fifth Amendment provides, in part: ". . . shall any person be . . . deprived of life, liberty, or property without due process of law."

> The Fourteenth Amendment reads as follows: Section 1. All persons born or naturalized in the United States, and subject to the jurisdiction thereof, are citizens of the United States and of the state wherein they reside. No state shall make or enforce any law which shall abridge the privileges or immunities of citizens of the United States, nor shall any state deprive any person of life, liberty, or property, without due process of law, nor deny to any person within its jurisdiction the equal protection of the laws.

There are two types of due process, namely *procedural due process* which means that one cannot be deprived of a right before given a notice of the charge against him and the necessary opportunity to defend himself; and *substantive due process* which requires that laws will operate equally with protection from arbitrary action. As a result of the historical decision in the *Gault* case, procedural due process has come into sharper focus in recent years.

1. *Hannah v. Larche*, 363 U.S. 420 (1960).

As indicated by an excerpt from the decision in this case, "procedural process" within the ambit of the

Fourteenth Amendment is difficult to define. Chief Justice Warren commented as follows:

> "Due process" is an elusive concept. Its exact boundaries are indefinable, and its content varies according to specific factual contexts. Thus when governmental agencies adjudicate or make binding determinations which directly affect the legal rights of individuals, it is imperative that those agencies use the procedures which have traditionally been associated with the judicial process. On the other hand, when governmental action does not partake of an adjudication, as for example, when a general fact-finding investigation is being conducted, it is not necessary that the full panoply of judicial procedures be used. Therefore, as a generalization, it can be said that due process embodies the differing rules of fair play, which through the years, have become associated with differing types of proceedings. Whether the Constitution requires that a particular right [be] obtain[ed] in a specific proceeding depends upon a complexity of factors. The nature of the alleged right involved, the nature of the proceeding, and the possible burden on that proceeding are all considerations which must be taken into account (*Id.* at 442).

2. *Gault, In re,* 387 U.S. 1 (1967).

In this precedential case it was revealed that Gerald Gault, a fifteen-year-old son was arrested because of an alleged obscene telephone call to a female neighbor. As a consequence he was immediately placed in a children's detention home. His parents, who were both at work away from home at the time, were not notified of their son's arrest.

After running the gamut of the lower court systems, it was finally carried to the United States Supreme Court where primary consideration was given as to whether a juvenile is a "delinquent" merely as a result of alleged misconduct on his part, with the consequence that he could be committed to a state institution.

The following excerpts of the lengthy ruling opinion are quoted as follows:

> From the inception of the juvenile court systems, wide differences have been tolerated — indeed insisted upon — between the procedural rights accorded to adults and those of juveniles. In practically all jurisdictions there are rights granted to adults which are withheld from juveniles . . . (*Id.* at 14).
>
> . . . A boy is charged with misconduct. The boy is committed to an institution where he may be restrained of liberty for years. It is of no constitutional consequence — and of limited practical meaning — that the Institution to which he is committed is called an Industrial School. The fact of the matter is that, however euphemistic the title, a "receiving home" or an "industrial school" for juveniles is an institution of confinement in which the child is incarcerated for a greater or lesser time. His world becomes "a building with whitewashed

walls, regimented routine and institutional hours. . . ." Instead of mother and father and sisters and brothers and friends and classmates, his world is peopled by guards, custodians, state employees, and "delinquents" confined with him for anything from waywardness to rape and homicide.

In view of this, it would be extraordinary if our Constitution did not require procedural regularity and the exercise of care implied in the phrase "due process." Under our Constitution, the condition of being a boy does not justify a kangaroo court (*Id.* at 27-8).

We conclude that the Due Process Clause of the Fourteenth Amendment requires that in respect of proceedings to determine delinquency which may result in commitment to an institution in which the juvenile's freedom is curtailed, the child and his parents must be notified of the child's rights to be represented by counsel, that counsel will be appointed to represent the child (*Id.* at 41).

In essence the Gault decision means that before a juvenile can be found guilty and penalized he must be accorded the same due process rights accorded adults, such as: (1) notice of the charges; (2) right to counsel; (3) right to confrontation and cross-examination of the witnesses; (4) privilege against self-incrimination; (5) right to transcript of the proceedings; and (6) right to appellate review.

3. *Sullivan v. Houston Independent School District,* 307 F. Supp. 1328 (S.D. Tex. 1969).

Notification of the charges is particularly important when youths are involved in serious disciplinary cases, as is emphasized in this case:

> The high school student perhaps even more than the university student needs careful adherence to concepts of procedural fairness and reasonableness by school officials. As minors they occupy a different status under the law and often are too inexperienced or immature to know how to protect themselves against charges of misconduct. Parents or guardians have legal obligations to children of high school age and common sense dictates that they should be included in any disciplinary action against their children which could result in severe punishment. Indeed it may be even more crucial that proper written notice of charges be provided to parents for often they do not know what has transpired at school. When severe discipline is contemplated — either expulsion or suspension for a substantial time — the student and his parents should be given ample time before the hearing to examine the charges, prepare a defense and gather evidence and witnesses, and it goes without saying that the disciplinary official should endeavor to maintain a neutral position until he has heard all of the facts (*Id.* at 1343).

4. *Cuff, In re*, No. 7816, Sept. 18, 1967, Decision of the N.Y. Commissioner of Education.

Right to counsel is enunciated by the Commissioner of Education in New York in a pupil suspension case:

Recent court decisions have indicated that administrative officers may unreasonably infringe upon rights which, had the minor been of age, would have been protected by safeguards in the form of a right to a full hearing with representation by counsel (*Id.* at 61).

Being a minor, the pupil is entitled to be questioned by the local authorities in the presence of his parents and at the parents' option, his attorney, who in turn must be given an opportunity to question the school personnel involved. In the context of today's society, to deprive a pupil permanently of a high school education is too serious an injury to the pupil, as well as potentially to society, to allow omission of basic safeguards of due process of law in ascertaining the true facts on which such action must be based, if it is to be taken at all (*Id.* at 62).

5. *In re Gault, supra.*

Justice Fortas made the following comments pertaining to the *right against self-incrimination*:

It would indeed be surprising if the privilege against self-incrimination were available to hardened criminals but not to children. The language of the Fifth Amendment, applicable to the States by operation of the Fourteenth Amendment, is unequivocal and without exception. (*Id.* at 47).

In fact, evidence is accumulating that confessions by juveniles do not aid in "individualized treatment," as the court below put it, and that compelling the child to answer questions, without warning or advice as to his right to remain silent, does not serve this or any other good purpose. . . . It seems probable that where children are induced to confess by "paternal" urgings on the part of officials and the confession is then followed by disciplinary action, the child's reaction is likely to be hostile and adverse — the child may well feel that he has been led or tricked into confession and that despite his confession, he is being punished (*Id.* at 51-2).

We conclude that the constitutional privilege against self-incrimination is applicable in the case of juveniles as it is with respect to adults. . . . If counsel was not present for some permissible reason when the admission was obtained, the greatest care must be taken to assure that the admission was voluntary, in the sense not only that it was not coerced or suggested, but also that it was not the product of ignorance of rights or of adolescent fantasy, fright or despair (*Id.* at 55).

6. *Conyers v. Pinellas County Board of Public Instruction*, Fla. Cir. Ct. No. 16, 1634 (1969).

The judiciary as well as school officials have indicated their annoyance with the claims of *light* disciplinary action taken in *minor* cases without *complete* conformance to *all* the rights of due process enumerated in the *Gault* opinion. Consequently, strict application of due process rights for pupils of all ages and for all offenses is receiving scrutinization and criticism. The *Conyers* case is, in point, where the litigated issue was "whether the public schools must accord due process of law — charges, notice of hearing, time to prepare for hearing, confrontation of witnesses, appeal, stay pending appeal — in enforcing the school regulations respecting hair length" (at 1).

The judge in this case pointed out the difficulties which would be encountered by school officials if pupils were granted due process in *all* matters of school discipline:

> Consider the chaos in our public schools if we are to permit seven-year-olds, and eleven-year-olds and fifteen-year-olds and seventeen-year-olds to demand notice, time to prepare for hearing, confrontation of witnesses, stay of judgment, and appeal each time a school official charges one with violation of a valid regulation and proposed approximate action. . . .
>
> Our public school authorities have had wished upon them much more than they have asked. This court will not impose upon them the impossible (*Id.* at 8).

7. *Farrell v. Joel*, 437 F.2d 160 (2d Cir. 1971).

This case also minimizes the adherence to procedural rights for pupils charged with misconduct. Litigation in the case developed from a "sit-in" by a girl which was a violation of a school rule. In commenting on the case, the court stated, in part:

Due process does not invariably require the procedural safeguards accorded in a criminal proceeding. Rather, "the very nature of due process negates any concept of inflexible procedures universally applicable to every imaginable situation" (*Id.* at 162).

Of course, as one approaches the center of the two extremes of major and minor discipline the line becomes shadowy, but the difficulty of drawing it does not eliminate the distinction between the two. Moreover, the general age level of the student group involved might affect determination of the constitutional issue. A "demonstration" in kindergarten, after all, is not the same as one in college (*Id.* at 163.)

Finally, in cases of minor discipline particularly, parent, student, and administrator should remember that substitution of common sense for zealous adherence to legal positions is not absolutely prohibited (*Id.* at 163).

8. *Sims v. Board of Education of Independent School District No. 22,* 329 F. Supp. 678 (N.M. 1971).

Misconduct sometimes requires immediate action, such as corporal punishment, without first resorting to formal due process procedures. For example, in the instant case, the court stated:

This court knows of no law which establishes the right of a school pupil to formal notice, hearing, or representation, before corporal punishment may be inflicted by school authorities. We find no reported case so holding and counsel have cited none. This Court takes judicial notice that the purposes to be served by corporal punishment would be long since passed if formal notice, hearing and representation were required (*Id.* at 683).

§ 4.3 Administration of corporal punishment.

Generally, in order for corporal punishment to be legal, it must be reasonable in the eyes of the judiciary. Ever since the beginning of litigation on the issue, the courts have generally held that if corporal punishment is to be inflicted upon pupils it should: (1) be in conformance with statutory enactment; (2) be for the purpose of correction without malice; (3) not be cruel or excessive so as to leave permanent marks or injuries; and (4) be suited to the age and sex of the pupil.

1. *State v. Pendergrass*, 19 N.C. 365, 31 Am. Dec. 416 (1837).

This early case established a principle which is still quite applicable to present-day cases in setting forth the limits in which corporal punishment may be administered. In rendering a decision in an action against a teacher for whipping a pupil so severely as to leave marks but leaving no permanent injury, the court expressed what it considered the proper rule of law:

> The line which separates moderate correction from immediate punishment can only be ascertained by reference to general principles. The welfare of the child is the main purpose for which pain is permitted to be

inflicted. Any punishment, therefore, which may seriously endanger life, limb, or health, or shall disfigure the child, or cause any other injury, may be pronounced in itself as immoderate, as not only being unnecessary for, but inconsistent with, the purpose for which correction is authorized. But any correction, however severe, which produces temporary pain only, and no permanent ill, cannot be so pronounced, since it may have been necessary for the reformation of the child, and does not injuriously affect its future welfare. We hold, therefore, that it may be laid down as a general rule, that teachers exceed the limits of their authority when they cause lasting mischief; but act within the limit of it when they inflict temporary pain (*Id.* at 417).

2. *State v. Thornton,* 136 N.C. 610, 48 S.E. 602 (1904). In another North Carolina case it was held that where moderation of punishment is a factor, the fact that an *excessive* beating may have a good effect on a pupil and the school, does *not* relieve the teacher of liability. Here an angered teacher improved the discipline in the school by *immoderately* whipping a pupil. In commenting on the case the court defined the following legal principle:

The good effect the chastisement of the prosecutor had upon the discipline of the school was manifestly irrelevant. Suppose the defendant had grievously wounded the prosecutor, or disfigured or maimed him, would such evidence be competent, and, if not in such a case, why should it be if the punishment was excessive and inflicted maliciously? The law does not tolerate evil that good may come. A teacher by his very excesses may inspire· terror in his pupils, and thus subdue them to his will and authority; but the law will not excuse his cruel acts for the sake of good discipline in his school (*Id.* at 603).

3. *Metcalf v. State*, 21 Tex. App. 174, 17 S.W. 142 (1886).

Although a teacher is generally restricted to inflict only moderate punishment, in certain instances he may be allowed to employ more violent measures if the circumstances necessitate such action. Such was the case when a pupil, over seventeen years of age and larger in size and weight than the teacher, came to school armed with a pistol and threatened to shoot the teacher when he asked for the gun. The court upheld the teacher for using a club for the purpose of disarming the pupil and ruled that the punishment administered was not excessive in that particular instance. In rendering a decision in favor of the teacher, the court said:

> If the force was not excessive, and, in our opinion, it was not, then appellant instead of being punished, should be commended in his efforts to maintain obedience, not only to the rules of the school, but to the laws of the state. That the pupil should have been punished for carrying a deadly weapon into the school in violation of the rules is, we think, beyond question (*Id.* at 143).

4. *Indiana State Personnel Board v. Jackson,* 244 Ind. 321, 192 N.E.2d 740 (1963).

As late as 1963, an Indiana court placed emphasis on the *in loco parentis* doctrine in upholding a teacher's resort to corporal punishment, and made the following comment:

> The law is well settled in this state that the teacher stands in loco parentis to the child, and her authority in this respect is no more subject to question than is the authority of the parent. The teacher's authority and the kind and quantum of punishment employed to meet a given offense is measured by the same rules, standards and requirements as fixed and established for parents (*Id.* at 744).

5. *Sims v. Board of Education of Independent School District No. 22,* 329 F. Supp. 678 (N.M. 1971).

The complaint in this case alleges that corporal punishment serves no legitimate educational purpose and "tends to inhibit learning, retard social growth and force acceptance of an inferior class position upon the plaintiff and other similarly situated members of his class"; "subject him to further humiliation because of the public or semi-public character of the act as it is practiced"; and that "the psychological harm done plaintiff and other members of class by the implication of corporal punishment is substantial and lasting" (*Id.* at 680-81).

In upholding the right of the school to exercise discretion in inflicting corporal punishment, the court pointed out that:

Corporal punishment by teachers was practiced in the schools long prior to the adoption of the Fourteenth Amendment. It has continued to be practiced since the adoption of the Equal Protection Clause ... (*Id.* at 687).

This Court cannot, under the applicable law, and would not if applicable law permitted the exercise of such discretion, substitute its judgment for the judgment of the defendants in the case at hand or what regulations are appropriate to maintain order and insure respect of pupils for school discipline and property. This Court will not act as a super school board to second guess the defendants. If acts violative of reasonable school regulations be not discouraged and punished, those acts can result in the disruption of the schools themselves. If our educational institutions are not allowed to rule themselves, within reasonable bounds, as here, experience has demonstrated that others will rule them to their destruction (*Id.* at 690).

6. *People v. Ball*, 58 Ill. 2d 36, 317 N.E.2d 54 (1974).

The case report indicates that an eleven-year-old boy who was obstreperous and defiant on the playground, was *severely* paddled by a teacher. The boy was taken to the hospital where the examining doctor

testified that it was one of the most severe paddling cases he had ever observed. ... The family physician testified that he ordered tranquilizers for the boy, who was emotionally distraught from the paddling. His mother also stated that the boy was very upset immediately after the incident and continued to become so whenever he saw the defendant (*Id.* at 55).

In finding the defendant guilty, the trial judge stated that while a teacher may administer "just and reasonable punishment — corporal punishment included" — maintaining discipline in the classroom, the defendant in this case inflicted corporal punishment more severe than the boy's parents would have had a right to administer. . . . The court further indicated that it did not intend to take the right of discipline away from the teacher who stands *in loco parentis* but rather to insure that such discipline is "just and reasonable" (*Id.* at 56).

We think it follows that teachers should be subject to the same standards of reasonableness which have long been applicable to parents in disciplining their children (*Id.* at 57).

7. *Roy v. Continental Insurance Company,* 313 So.2d 349 (La. App. 1975).

This case typifies other recent cases where, in the absence of statutory prohibition, corporal punishment may be inflicted upon unruly students if reasonably applied. (The Louisiana statutes do not explicitly establish the right of a teacher to use corporal punishment but then neither do they prohibit same.)

Here a teacher separated and reprimanded two boys for fighting. Upon release Roy (the plaintiff) cursed the teacher, calling him a "God-damn son of a bitch" and threatened reprisal by his father.

This aggravation prompted the teacher to apply a wooden paddle to the eighth-grade student's posterior and give him several swats.

When the case reached the Court of Appeals, the ruling was in favor of the teacher. The court defended its decision with the following well-stated comments:

> The use of corporal punishment as discipline by teachers apparently stems from the age old principle that a schoolmaster is regarded as standing in "loco parentis" or in the shoes of a parent while the child is attending school, and as a result shares in the right to demand and obtain obedience from the student. Thus parental authority has been deemed to be delegated to the teacher. Insofar as the type or form of discipline is concerned, it must be conceded that parents have the right to inflict corporal punishment upon their children, subject of course to the limitation of jeopardizing the health or safety of the child. This court is of the opinion that teachers likewise have this limited right. Without doubt, some children of school age are immature, undisciplined, rebellious, and have a self-serving inability to recognize the necessity for regulation. As a result disruptive conduct often occurs. A teacher has the duty of maintaining discipline and good order in our schools, in addition to being responsible for the progress, conduct, and education of our

children. In order for these educators to discharge this duty and maintain orderly conduct of activities in the classroom and on the school grounds, we opine they must be given the means of enforcing prompt discipline, one such means being reasonable corporal punishment. A general rule to the negative, insofar as corporal punishment is concerned would in our minds "encourage students to flaunt the authority of their teachers," and effectively shackle the teaching profession at a time of rising disciplinary problems in our schools (*Id.* at 553-54).

8. *Baker v. Owen,* 395 F. Supp. 294 (M.D.N.C.); 423 U.S. 907, 96 S. Ct. 210 (1975).

This case reached the United States Supreme Court for final settlement. It involved a mild paddling administered to a sixth-grade student, which resulted in a suit, instituted by Mrs. Baker, the boy's mother, claiming illegality of the corporal punishment *over parental objection.* She argued that the North Carolina statute which empowers school officials to "use reasonable force in the exercise of lawful authority to restrain or correct pupils and to maintain order" is unconstitutional insofar as it allows corporal punishment over parental objection.

The court was not convinced by the argument as evidenced by its following statement:

It should be clear beyond peradventure, indeed self-evident, that to fulfill its assumed duty of providing an education to all who want it, a state must maintain order within its schools. . . . So long as the force used is reasonable — and that is all that the statute here allows — school officials are free to employ corporal punishment for disciplinary purposes until in the exercise of their own professional judgment, or in response to concerted pressure from opposing parents, they decide that its harm outweighs its utility (*Id.* at 301).

The *Baker* case was appealed to the United States Supreme Court where on October 20, 1975, it affirmed without comment, the decision of the federal district court.

9. *Ingraham v. Wright,* 525 F.2d 909 (5th Cir. 1976), *aff'd,* 97 S. Ct. 1401 (1977).

In this case action was brought by parents of public school students seeking compensation and punitive damages and declaratory and injunctive relief with respect to use of corporal punishment in school systems.

Plaintiff-appellant (Ingraham) alleged that the infliction of corporal punishment on public school children on its face, and as applied in the instant case, constitutes "cruel and unusual punishment under the Eighth Amendment" sufficient to entitle plaintiffs to damages and injunctive relief. To this charge the court responded thusly:

We do not agree. It is the opinion of the majority of this court that the Eighth Amendment does not apply to the administration of discipline, through corporal punishment, to public school children by public school teachers and administrators (*Id.* at 912).

We do not mean to imply by our holding that we condone child abuse, either in the home or the schools. We abhor any exercise of discipline which would result in serious or permanent injury to the child. Indeed if the force used by defendant teachers in disciplining plaintiff was as severe as plaintiffs allege, a Florida state court could find defendants civilly and criminally liable for tortious conduct exceeding the level of severity authorized by Florida statute and Dade County School Board policy (*Id.* at 915).

10. *Jackson v. Bishop,* 404 F.2d 571 (8th Cir. 1968).

There is judicial authority asserting that corporal punishment violates the Eighth Amendment. For example, in *Jackson,* Judge (now Justice) Blackmun stated that: "corporal punishment offends contemporary concepts of decency and human dignity and precepts of civilization which we profess to possess" (*Id.* at 579).

11. *Cooper v. McJunkin,* 4 Ind. 290 (1853).

The administration of corporal punishment for pupils was denounced over a century ago, as indicated by the following classic statement of Judge Stuart:

In one respect the tendency of the rod is so evidently evil, that it might, perhaps be arrested on the ground of public policy. The practice has an inherent proneness to abuse. The very act of whipping engenders passion, and very generally leads to excess (*Id.* at 292).

It can hardly be doubted but that public opinion will in time, strike the ferule from the hands of the teacher leaving him as the true basis of government, only the resources of his intellect and heart. Such is the only policy worthy of the state, and of the otherwise enlightened and liberal institutions. It is the policy of progress. The husband can no longer moderately chastise his wife; nor, according to more recent authorities, the master his servant or apprentice. Even the degrading cruelties of the naval service have been arrested. Why the person of the school-boy, "with his shining morning face," should be less sacred in the eyes of the law than that of the apprentice or the sailor, is not easily explained. It is regretted that such are the authorities — still courts are bound by them (*Id.* at 292-93).

§ 4.4 Suspension and expulsion.

The legal principle is firmly established that school authorities may *suspend* or *expel* from school any student who disobeys a reasonable rule or regulation within statutory limits. With the alarming increase of student misbehavior in the public schools today, and the diminution of corporal punishment as a means of abating the misbehaviors, school authorities often exercise their prerogative to employ the alternatives of suspension and expulsion.

1. *Pugsley v. Sellmeyer,* 158 Ark. 247, 250 S.W. 538 (1923).

As illustrated by this case, school authorities suspended or expelled students for rather "trivial" reasons several decades ago. Moreover, the courts were reluctant to intervene with school-board actions.

Here the Supreme Court of Arkansas upheld expulsion of a student for violation of a rule against the use of cosmetics. The court's rationale for non-interference is expressed as follows:

> The question, therefore, is not whether we approve this rule as one we would have made as directors of the district, nor are we required to find whether it was essential to the maintenance of discipline. On the contrary, we must uphold the rule unless we find that the directors have clearly abused their discretion, and that the rule is not one reasonably calculated to effect the purpose intended, that is, of promoting discipline in the school; and we do not so find.
>
> Courts have other and more important functions to perform than that of hearing the complaints of disaffected pupils of the public schools against rules and regulations promulgated by the school boards for the government of the schools. . . . These directors are in close and intimate touch with the affairs of their respective districts, and know the conditions with which they have to deal. It will be remembered also that respect for constituted authority and obedience thereto is an essential lesson to qualify one for the duties of citizenship, and that the schoolroom is an

appropriate place to teach that lesson; so that the courts hesitate to substitute their will and judgment for that of the school boards which are delegated by law as the agencies to prescribe rules for the government of the public schools of the state, which are supported at public expense (*Id.* at 539).

2. *Fortman v. Texarkana School District No. 7*, 514 S.W.2d 720 (Sup. Ct. of Ark. 1974).

Despite the reluctance of school officials to impose, and judges to approve, expulsion as a disciplinary measure, there are instances in which a pupil's misconduct is of such a grave nature that his or her presence is so disruptive and dangerous to the school, and detrimental to the morale of the student body that *expulsion* would likely be judicially condoned.

A good illustration of this legal principle is provided by this Arkansas case where a school board expelled two tenth-grade girls who deliberately planned and attacked a fellow pupil, following a verbal controversy at a dance attended by the students. The girl victim of the attack "was kicked, beaten, and stabbed twice in the head with a six-inch pair of scissors. Her injuries were serious but not fatal" (*Id.* at 721).

Counsel for the appellants argued that the board could not legally expel a student "beyond the current term" as stipulated in an Arkansas statute. The court refused to accept such a narrow interpretation of the statute, and upheld the board's action, with the following supportive statement:

141

... school directors are authorized, not only to exercise the powers that are expressly granted by statutes, but also such powers as may be fairly implied therefrom, and from the duties which are expressly imposed upon them. Such powers will be implied when the exercise thereof is clearly necessary to enable them to carry out and perform the duties legally imposed upon them. Our school laws unquestionably impose upon school boards the duty of providing orderly education institutions. Scant imagination is required to think of innumerable situations in which the power of expulsion might be the school board's only effective means of protecting the student body from the disruptive, violent, or criminal actions of an incorrigibly intractable pupil (*Id.* at 722).

3. *Cook v. Edwards,* 341 F. Supp. 307 (D.N.H. 1972). School officials usually impose severe penalties on students who show signs of intoxication. Such was true in the instant case, where a fifteen-year-old female student admittedly appeared at school in an intoxicated condition, the consequence of which was dismissal from school.

In questioning the severity of the *indefinite* dismissal, the judge made the following remarks on the basis of substantive due process:

However, the punishment of indefinite expulsion raises a serious question as to substantive due process. The result of indefinite expulsion may be the end of the plaintiff's scholastic career either because of its long continuance or because the plaintiff herself will decide to end the uncertainty of punishment by quitting school entirely. . . . I can see good and sufficient reasons why a pupil who appears drunk on the school premises should be expelled from school for a definite period of time, or even permanently, if the circumstances warrant it, but I perceive no valid reason for making the expulsion indefinite. . . . My concern is the plaintiff's constitutional rights. If judges, and particularly federal judges, were to tailor their decisions as to what they thought the public wanted, the rule of law and the protection that the Constitution affords would soon vanish (*Id.* at 311).

4. *Goss v. Lopez,* 95 S. Ct. 729 (Ohio 1975).

For some years the lower federal courts had been struggling over the question as to how long a student could be expelled from school without first being afforded all the formal procedures of due process. Finally the United States Supreme Court attempted to bring the issue to rest.

It held that students suspended for *short periods* of time were nevertheless entitled to minimal due process under the Fourteenth Amendment. In essence, the ruling struck down an Ohio law which authorized school officials to suspend a student for ten days or less without giving the student advance notice of the charges against him and without affording him the opportunity to defend himself.

Justice White, who wrote for the majority, described what it considered a proper hearing in a suspension case in the following terms:

The difficulty is that our schools are vast and complex. Some modicum of discipline and order is essential if the educational function is to be performed. Events calling for discipline are frequent occurrences and sometimes require immediate, effective action. Suspension is considered not only to be a necessary tool to maintain order but a valuable educational device. The prospect of imposing elaborate hearing requirements in every suspension case is viewed with great concern, and many school authorities may well prefer the untrammeled power to act unilaterally, unhampered by rules about notice and hearing. But it would be a strange disciplinary system in an educational institution if no communication was sought by the disciplinarian with the student in an effort to inform him of his defalcation and to let him tell his side of the story in order to make sure that an injustice is not done (*Id.* at 739).

We do not believe that school authorities must be totally free from notice and hearing requirements if their schools are to operate with acceptable efficiency. Students facing temporary suspension have interests qualifying for protection of the Due Process Clause, and due process requires, in connection with a suspension of ten days or less, that the student be given oral or written notice of the charges against him and, if he denies them, an explanation of the evidence the authorities have and an opportunity to present his side of the story. The clause requires at least these rudimentary precautions against unfair or mistaken findings of misconduct and arbitrary exclusion from school (*Id.* at 739-40).

Because of the split 5-4 decision, it is logical to assume there were strong arguments in the *minority opinion*, written by Justice Powell. Part of the dissenting opinion follows:

The Court today invalidates an Ohio statute that permits student suspensions from school without a hearing "for not more than ten days." The decision unnecessarily opens avenues for judicial intervention in the operation of our public schools that may affect adversely the quality of education. The Court holds for the first time that the federal courts, rather than educational officials and state legislatures, have the authority to determine the rules applicable to routine classroom discipline of children and teenagers in the public schools. It justifies this unprecedented intrusion into the process of elementary and secondary education by identifying a new constitutional right: the right of a student not to be suspended for as much as a single day without notice and due process hearing either before or promptly following the suspension (*Id.* at 741).

If, as seems apparent, the Court will now
require due process procedures, whenever
such routine school decisions are challenged,
the impact upon public education will be
serious indeed. The discretion and judgment of
federal courts across the land often will be
substituted for that of the 50-state
legislatures, and 14,000 school boards and the
2,000,000 teachers who heretofore have been
responsible for the administration of the
American public school system. If the Court
perceives a national and analytically sound
distinction between the discretionary decision
by school authorities to suspend a pupil for a
brief period, and the types of discretionary
school decisions described above, it would be
prudent to articulate it in today's opinion.
Otherwise, the federal courts should prepare
themselves for a vast new role in society (*Id.* at
748-49).

5. *Wood v. Strickland,* 95 S. Ct. 992 (Ark. 1975).

As in *Lopez,* this case also received national attention
and concern. Facts of the case revealed that a couple of
sixteen-year-old girls in the tenth grade "spiked" the
punch which was to be served to an extra-curricular
school organization attended by parents and students.
Since this was in violation of school regulations, the
"prank" resulted in expulsion from school.

When the case finally reached the United States
Supreme Court, it was held that (1) the girls had not
been accorded due process of law and (2) school board
members, as individuals, are not immune from liability

for compensating damages under the Civil Rights Act of 1871.

With respect to the pertinent issue of *absolute* immunity of individual school board members, the court stated:

> Absolute immunity would not be justified since it would not sufficiently increase the ability of school officials to exercise their discretion in a forthright manner to warrant the absence of a remedy for students subjected to intentional or otherwise inexcusable deprivations (*Id.* at 1000).
>
> . . . The official must himself be acting sincerely and with a belief that he is doing right, but an act violating a student's constitutional rights can be no more justified by ignorance or disregard of settled, indisputable law on the part of one entrusted with supervision of students' daily lives than by the presence of actual malice be entitled to a special exemption. . . . Therefore, in the specific context of school discipline, we hold that a school board member is not immune from liability for damages . . . if he knew or reasonably should have known that the action he took within his sphere of official responsibility could violate the constitutional rights of the student affected, or if he took the action with the malicious intention to cause a deprivation of constitutional rights or other injury to the student . . . (*Id.* at 1000-1001).

The four *dissenting* judges in this case expressed their concern about the injurious effects the decision might have upon the future procuring of school board members in the following excerpt:

> There are some 20,000 school boards, each with five or more members, and thousands of school superintendents and school principals. More of the school board members are popularly elected, drawn from the citizenry at large, and possess no unique competency in divining the law. Few cities and counties provide any compensation for service on school boards, and often it is difficult to persuade qualified persons to assume the burdens of this important function in our society. Moreover, even if counsel's advice constitutes a defense, it may safely be assumed that few school boards and school officials have ready access to counsel on the countless decisions that necessarily must be made in the operation of our public schools (*Id.* at 1005).

6. *Lee v. Mason County Board of Education,* 490 F.2d 458 (5th Cir. 1974).

The judiciary agrees that the behavior of some students is so disruptive and dangerous that school boards are legally justified in separating them from other students by long-term suspension or even expulsion. The courts emphasize, however, that such action carries with it the responsibility to find suitable alternatives for regular school attendance. A statement in the opinion of a federal court is illustrative:

... a sentence of banishment from the educational system is, insofar as the institution has power to act, the extreme penalty, the ultimate· punishment. In our increasing technological society getting at least a high school education is almost necessary for survival. Stripping a child of access to educational opportunity is a life sentence to second rate citizenship, unless the child has the financial ability to migrate to another school system or enter private school (*Id.* at 460).

7. *"R. K." v. Board of Education of the Township of Lakewood* (Decision of the N.J. Commissioner of Education, June 19, 1973).

The New Jersey Commissioner of Education has ruled upon numerous cases involving expulsions and long-time suspensions, in which he frequently mentions the school board's responsibility in seeing that the excluded student is not deprived of further educational opportunity. An excerpt from the instant case is illustrative:

Termination of a pupil's right to attend the public schools of a district is a drastic and desperate remedy which should be employed only when no other course is possible. . . . It is obvious that a board of education cannot wash its hands of a problem by recourse to expulsion, while such an act may resolve an immediate problem for the school, it may likewise create a host of others involving not only the pupil but the community and society at large. The Commissioner suggests, therefore, that boards of education who are found to take expulsion action cannot shrug off responsibility but should make every effort to see that the child comes under the aegis of another agency able to deal with the problem. The Commissioner urges boards of education, therefore, to recognize expulsion as a negative and defeatist kind of last-ditch expedient resorted to only after and based upon competent professional evaluation and recommendation.

§ 4.5 Deprivation of awards and privileges.

1. *Valentine v. Independent School District of Casey,* 191 Iowa 1100, 183 N.W. 434 (1921).

This early case involved exclusion from graduation ceremonies for infraction of school board directives.

According to the case report, last-minute directions from the school board demanded that "caps and gowns should be worn on that auspicious occasion, and the same were furnished by the board." Three of six girls, who were to have graduated, refused to wear the caps which were misfits or because of their offensive odor emanating from recent fumigation with formaldehyde. Consequently the defiant "girls who were not permitted to occupy seats on the platform and [to whom] diplomas were not granted" (*Id.* at 435).

In holding for a student, who had established a high academic record, the court stated:

The issuance of a diploma by the school board to a pupil who satisfactorily completed the prescribed course of study and who is otherwise qualified is mandatory, and, although such duty is not expressly enjoined upon the board by statute, it does arise by necessary and reasonable implication (*Id.* at 437).

2. *Ladson v. Board of Education of Union Free School District No. 9*, 323 N.Y.S.2d 545 (Sup. Ct., 1971).

This case grew out of an incident where a senior black girl was excluded from participating in the graduation ceremonies because of an alleged assault on the high school principal. As a consequence she was refused the privilege to participate in the graduation ceremony.

After failing to find statutory authority to school officials to take such action the court held for the girl and stated its rationale for doing so in the following paragraph:

The Court is persuaded that punishment and discipline should be responsive to the educational goals to which the school system is dedicated. Courts are dedicated not only to the administration of laws, but to the pursuit of justice, and the two ideals must come together. The justice of the situation favors graduation attendance. We have here a student of demonstrated dedication, who has persevered through all of her term in high school and has completed her final year under adversity, even though some of that adversity may be of her own doing. She has been accepted at college. Her graduation ceremony is important and

meaningful to her personally and in her family
which has never before had a high school
graduate. She has no other record of disorder
than the one incident here involved. It would
indeed be a distortion of our educational
process in this period of youthful
discontentment to snatch from a young woman
at the point of educational fruition the
savoring of her educational success. The Court
believes that not to be a reasonable
punishment meant to encourage the best
educational results (*Id.* at 550).

3. *Dorsey v. Bale*, 521 S.W.2d 76 (Ky. Ct. of App.
1975).

Courts frown upon reduction of grades as a punitive
measure. This illustrative case grew out of a contested
regulation in the school's Handbook which provided
that:

> Absences for any other reason and failure to
> follow the outlined procedure will constitute an
> unexcused absence and work will not be
> allowed to be made up and furthermore five (5)
> points will be deducted from the total
> nine-week grades for each unexcused absence
> from each class during the grading period (*Id.*
> at 77).

Bale had his *grades reduced* for unexcused absences
as an additional punishment leading to his suspension
from classes. The Board argued that it had the
statutory authority to "do all things necessary to
accomplish the purpose for which it was created" and

was therefore authorized to "make and adopt rules and regulations for the conduct of pupils."

That argument did not prevent the court from declaring the regulation to be invalid. It ruled that the contested statute authorizing suspension or expulsion for misconduct did not authorize the lowering of grades as a punitive measure. In support of its decision the court remarked:

> We are of the opinion that this statute, under which Tommy Bale was suspended, clearly preempts the right of school officials to promulgate disciplinary regulations that impose additional punishment for the conduct that results in suspension. If the conduct of the student in the judgment of the school authorities warrants invoking the statutory authority to suspend, they have the right to determine the duration of suspension so that such action constitutes a complete punishment for the offense (*Id.* at 78).

§ 4.6 Humiliation as a punitive measure.

Some teachers can concoct disciplinary practices which are more objectionable than mere corporal punishment. Humiliation of a student before his classmates can be more deleterious than the infliction of physical pain.

1. *Celestine v. Lafayette Parish School Board*, 284 So.2d 650 (La. 1973).

This case confirms the above-stated principle, where a teacher was dismissed for requiring pupils to write a "vulgar word" 1,000 times in the presence of their classmates, as a disciplinary measure for having uttered the word. The case report reads as follows:

> Shortly after his class reconvened following the noon lunch period on the above mentioned date, plaintiff was confronted by several students who told him that two of his girl students had been using "bad words." Plaintiff thereupon asked the two girls in the presence of other members of the class whether they had been using vulgar language, and when they responded that they had, he instructed each of them to write the vulgar word 1,000 times and to turn that work in to the principal for his signature, and to the parents for their signatures. One of the two girls to whom the assignment was given was eleven years of age at that time.
>
> Pursuant to his instruction given to them by plaintiff, each of these girls began writing a four-lettered word, beginning with the letter "F," being an extremely vulgar word meaning sexual intercourse. They spent the rest of that day carrying out the assignment of writing that word 1,000 times . . . (*Id.* at 652).

As a consequence the teacher was dismissed by the board of education and the dismissal was upheld by the court, with the following reason:

> We do not believe that the right of academic freedom entitles a public school teacher to require his students, particularly very young people, to use and be exposed to vulgar words,

particularly when no academic or educational purpose can possibly be served. In the instant suit, we agree with the School Board and the trial court that plaintiff did not have the right, under the principle of academic freedom or any other theory, to require an eleven-year-old girl to write the very vulgar word which was involved here even once, when no valid purpose conceivably could be served by the use of that word. He certainly had no right to require her to write such a word many times in the presence of her classmates. His very poor judgment in imposing such a requirement is sufficient to support the action of the School Board in dismissing him (*Id.* at 655).

Part II

COURT CASES INVOLVING THE TEACHER

PRELUDE

As a prelude to the chapters which are included in Part II (Court Cases Involving the Teacher), the following introductory passage is quoted from the author's text, "Teachers' Legal Rights, Restraints and Liabilities":

A public school teacher possesses certain rights and freedoms enjoyed by all citizens. As a citizen he has the legal right to speak, think, and believe as he wishes. As a public school teacher, however, he must exercise these and other legal rights with due consideration of the effects upon others — particularly school children. Moreover, by virtue of his position, performing a governmental function, he must conform to certain laws, rules, and regulations not equally applicable to the ordinary citizen.

Those who enter the teaching profession should realize in advance that certain legal restrictions and requirements of the teacher are essential for the welfare of the social order. But when the restrictions and requirements appear to be unnecessary, unreasonable, or in conflict with constitutional guarantees, a teacher is privileged to stand up for his legal rights.

Obviously there may be a lack of agreement among teachers, school boards, legislatures and others as to what constitutes "reasonable"

157

and "constitutional" restrictions. When the disagreement develops into litigation, the courts determine the reasonableness and constitutionality of the statutory and school board restrictions concerning the teachers' rights, restraints and liabilities.

It is difficult to delineate precisely the rights from the restraints. Virtually all rights afforded teachers have limitations. Even rights stipulated in the statutes and constitution are not absolute as they pertain to teachers. The rights may be exercised only under certain conditions such as determined by place, time and manner. Generally, the courts will hold that the degree to which a teacher may exercise a right will depend upon the effect it would have upon his pupils (p. 1).

Chapter 5
RIGHT OF ASSOCIATION

§ 5. 1 Early judicial vacillation regarding affiliation with subversive organizations.

The most stringent and litigious law designed to purge the school system of subversive teachers was the Feinberg Law of New York State. Specifically the Feinberg Law provided that the Board of Regents, which has charge of the public school system of the state, shall, after full notice and hearing, make a listing of organizations which it finds advocate, advise, teach or embrace the doctrine that the government should be overthrown by force, violence, or any other unlawful means. The statute then authorized the Board of Regents to provide, by rule, that membership in any listed organization, after notice and hearing, "shall constitute prima facie evidence for disqualification for appointment to or retention in any office or position in the school system" (*New York Education Law,* Title V, Article 61, Sec. 3022 [effective July 1, 1949]).

Contemporaneously, the *Ober Law* was passed by the Maryland State Legislature for the same purpose — to ferret out teachers affiliated with subversive organizations. The *Ober Law* provided that:

> ... every [school] board shall establish ... procedures designed to ascertain before any person, including teachers and other

159

employees of any public educational institution in this State, is appointed or employed, that he or she as the case may be, is not a subversive person, and that there are no reasonable grounds to believe such persons are subversive persons. In the event such reasonable grounds exist, he or she as the case may be, shall not be appointed or employed. In securing any facts necessary to ascertain the information herein required, the applicant shall be required to sign a written statement containing answers to such inquiries as may be material, which statement shall contain notice that it is subject to the penalties of perjury (*Laws of Maryland,* 1949, Chapter 86, Article 11).

1. *L'Hommedieu v. Board of Regents,* 196 Misc. 686, 93 N.Y.S.2d 274 (1949).

Shortly after the enactment of the Feinberg Law, its constitutionality was challenged. A lower court agreed that the law was unconstitutional, declaring that:

> In the opinion of the court, this statute fails entirely in establishing a definite standard of prescribed conduct. It is a "dragnet which may enmesh anyone who agitates for a change of government" (93 N.Y.S.2d at 289).

> In reaching such conclusion, the Court is not, of course, oblivious to the practices of international Communism, which have met with such universal and well merited contempt among free men. It is not because they disapproved the evil thinkers and evil doers of their day less, but because they cherished their

democracy more, that the great makers and interpreters of our constitution have so jealously guarded the basic concepts of freedom.

It is no answer to say that this measure is needed to combat the menace of Communism. Small service, indeed, to our democracy, is afforded by emulating the tactics of Communism, and by destroying the guarantees of freedom (*Id.* at 293).

The court finds it hard to believe that it is necessary to resort to witch hunting in our schools to displace misfits. Necessary or not, the Feinberg Law cannot be the solution, because it is an answer which the Legislature, under the Constitution, is powerless to provide (*Id.* at 294).

2. *Thompson v. Wallin,* 95 N.Y.S.2d 784 (1950).

The decision in *L'Hommedieu,* as well as in this companion case, was immediately appealed to the Appellate Division where the decision of the lower court was reversed.

Judge Heffernan was emphatic in declaring the Feinberg Law constitutional and denunciating the contention of the plaintiff. His classic statement was to be accepted as the legal principle for years to come:

We are not dealing here with the propaganda of soap box orators, or the utterances of those who preach from housetops or pray on street corners. We are dealing with a statute pertaining solely to teachers whose influence upon the children who come under their instruction is extraordinary. It is, therefore, of paramount importance that the association of teacher and pupil should imbue the latter with love of country, respect for its laws and should inculcate in the childish mind principles of justice and patriotism. We are not so naive as to accept as gospel the argument that a teacher who believes in the destruction of our form of government will not affect his students (95 N.Y.S. [2d] at 453).

It is a fallacy to suppose that the state is so impotent, so helpless, that it is powerless to ban from its public schools traitorous instructors who preach and teach seditious doctrines with the sinister intent of destroying the constitution which they have sworn to support. It is an arrogant assumption that the government cannot protect itself against the infiltration of those who desire to destroy it by force (*Id.* at 456).

3. *Dworken v. Cleveland Board of Education,* 94 N.E.2d 18 (Ohio 1950).

It should not be inferred that a board of education is powerless to eliminate subversive persons from the teaching staff without expressed statutory or constitutional provisions to that effect. The permissive authority of boards of education in this respect was illustrated in *Dworken* where action was brought against the Cleveland Board of Education to enjoin the board from enforcing and carrying out a resolution requiring the signing of "loyalty" affidavits and oaths.

The plaintiff in the case was not a teacher. He merely complained on behalf of those whose "sensibilities" might be offended.

The affidavit which each school employee was required to execute before a notary public reads as follows:

> I do not advocate nor am I a member of any organization that advocates the overthrow of the Government of the United States of America by force, violence, or other unconstitutional means. . . . I do further swear (or affirm) I will not so advocate, nor will I become a member of such organization during the period that I am an employee (member) of the Cleveland Board of Education (*Id.* at 20).

The Ohio Court of Common Pleas, Connell J., held that the resolution did not violate the Constitution of the United States or the State of Ohio.

That the judicial lash was not spared in showing contempt for those who seek shelter under the Constitution, while attempting at the same time to abuse it, is reflected in the following excerpts from the court's opinion:

> The Cleveland Board of Education ... has not legally violated any one of our sacred instruments. The only thing it has violated is the sensibilities of those who do not wish their treachery in embryo to be noticed; because those who would create danger to our nation are incensed whenever their motives are exposed (*Id.* at 24).

It would seem to this Court that a Board of Education might very properly consider that the moulding of the minds of its youth, as well as the safety and perpetuation of the nation we inherited, are not to be outweighed by any consideration of the so-called "sensibilities" of those who would overthrow us (*Id.* at 26).

With the right of the Board to express tribute to our Constitution we shall not interfere; with its right, power, and duty to accept such expression from its teachers, we shall not interfere.

Such expressions never harmed the sensibilities of the Presidents, Governors, Senators, Congressmen, Judges, Mayors or other public officers privileged to take them, nor will they harm the teachers whose precept[s] and good example will influence the future public officers who take them (*Id.* at 32).

§ 5.2 Adler at the crossroads.

1. *Adler v. Board of Education of City of New York,* 342 U.S. 485, 72 S. Ct. 380 (1952).

This famous case was litigated immediately following enactment of the Feinberg Law. In brief, the issue in the case was whether a Civil Service Law of New York, implemented by the Feinberg Law, makes ineligible for employment in any public school any member of any organization advocating the overthrow of the Government by force, violence or any unlawful means.

Adler and several other teachers were dismissed from their positions by the New York City Board of

Education for their refusal to comply with the oath requirement involving the Feinberg Law. This set off litigation that continued through the entire judicial hierarchy, finally ending up in the United States Supreme Court which ruled against Adler, thereby sustaining the New York Law and the school board's action in dismissing teachers who violated the antisubversive law.

Justice Minton, speaking for the majority of the court, which was divided six to three, stated in part:

> It is clear that such persons have the right under our law to assemble, speak, think and believe as they will.... It is equally clear that they have no right to work for the State in the school system on their own terms. They may work for the school system upon the reasonable terms laid down by the proper authorities of New York. If they do not choose to work on such terms, they are at liberty to retain their beliefs and associations and go elsewhere. Has the State thus deprived them of any right to free speech or assembly? We think not ... (342 U.S. at 492).

> A teacher works in a sensitive area in a schoolroom. There he shapes the attitude of young minds towards the society in which they live. In this, the state has a vital concern. It must preserve the integrity of the schools. That the school authorities have the right and the duty to screen the officials, teachers, and employees as to their fitness to maintain the integrity of the schools as a part of ordered

society, cannot be doubted. One's associates, past and present, as well as one's conduct, may properly be considered in determining fitness and loyalty. From time immemorial one's reputation has been determined in part by the company he keeps. In the employment of officials and teachers of the school system, the state may very properly inquire into the company they keep, and we know of no rule, constitutional or otherwise, that prevents the state, when determining the fitness and loyalty of such persons, from considering the organizations and persons with whom they associate.

If, under the procedure set up in the New York law, a person is found to be unfit and is disqualified from employment in the public school system because of membership in a listed organization, he is not thereby denied the right of free speech and assembly. His freedom of choice between membership in the organization and employment in the school system might be limited, but not his freedom of speech or assembly, except in the remote sense that limitation is inherent in every choice. Certainly such limitation is not one the state may not make in the exercise of its police power to protect the schools from pollution and thereby to defend its own existence (342 U.S. at 493).

Of the three dissents, the one expressed by Douglas is particularly significant because of the later support it received by other courts, as well as the general public. In fact, it was a portent of a complete turnabout from the decisions rendered in the preceding cases dealing with the issue. Justice Douglas stated, in part:

> I have not been able to accept the recent doctrine that a citizen who enters the public service can be forced to sacrifice his civil rights. I cannot for example find in our constitutional scheme the power of a state to place its employees in the category of second-class citizens by denying their freedom of thought and expression. The Constitution guarantees freedom of thought and expression to everyone in our society. All are entitled to it; and none needs it more than the teacher.
>
> The public school is in most respects the cradle of our democracy. The increasing role of the public school is seized upon by proponents of the type of legislation represented by New York's Feinberg Law as proof of the importance and need for keeping the school free of "subversive influences." But that is to misconceive the effect of this type of legislation. Indeed the impact of this kind of censorship on the public school system illustrates the high purpose of the First Amendment in freeing speech and thought from censorship (*Id.* at 508).
>
> The very threat of such a procedure is certain to raise havoc with academic freedom. Youthful indiscretions, mistaken causes, misguided enthusiasm — all long forgotten —

becomes the ghosts of a harrowing present. Any organization committed to a liberal cause, any group organized to revolt against an hysterical trend, any committee launched to sponsor an unpopular program becomes suspect. These are the organizations into which Communists often infiltrate. Their presence infects the whole, even though the project was not conceived in sin. A teacher caught in that mesh is almost certain to stand condemned. Fearing condemnation, she will tend to shrink from any association that stirs controversy. In that manner freedom of expression will be stifled (*Id.* at 509).

§ 5.3 Judicial repudiation of the oath requirement.

1. *Elfbrandt v. Russell* (Ariz.), 384 U.S. 11, 87 S. Ct. 1238 (1966).

This case concerned the constitutionality of an Arizona Act requiring an oath from state employees (including public school teachers) that they were not knowingly members of the Communist Party or any other subversive organization. The oath reads as follows:

I do solemnly swear that I will support the Constitution of the United States and the Constitution and laws of the State of Arizona, that I will bear true faith and allegiance to the same, and defend them against all enemies, foreign and domestic, and that I will faithfully and impartially discharge the duties of the office (name of office) according to the best of my ability, so help me God (or so I do affirm).

168

A petitioner, a teacher and a Quaker, decided she could not, "in good conscience," take the oath, not knowing what it meant and being unable to obtain a hearing to determine its precise scope and meaning.

The Arizona Supreme Court sustained the oath, but when the case went to the United States Supreme Court, the ruling of the Arizona Supreme Court was overturned. Justice Douglas, who was joined by Chief Justice Warren and Justices Black, Brennan and Fortas, delivered the opinion for the majority, excerpts from which follow:

> The oath and accompanying statutory gloss challenged here suffer from an identical constitutional infirmity. One who subscribes to this Arizona oath and who is, or thereafter becomes a knowing member of an organization which has as "one of its purposes" the violent overthrow of the government, is subject to immediate discharge and criminal penalties. Nothing in the oath, the statutory gloss, or the construction of the oath and statutes given by the Arizona Supreme Court, purports to exclude association by one who does not subscribe to the organization's unlawful ends (384 U. S. at 16).

> Those who join an organization but do not share its unlawful purposes and who do not participate in its unlawful activities surely pose no threat, either as citizens or as public employees. Laws such as this which are not restricted in scope to those who join with the

"specific intent" to further illegal action impose, in effect, a conclusive presumption that the member shares the unlawful aims of the organization (*Id.* at 17).

A law which applies to membership without the "specific intent" to further the illegal aims of the organization infringes unnecessarily on protected freedoms. It rests on the doctrine of "guilt by association" which has no place here. Such a law cannot stand (*Id.* at 19).

Justice White, with whom Justices Clark, Harlan and Stewart concurred, wrote a dissenting opinion which concluded with the following comment:

Even if Arizona may not take criminal action against its law enforcement officers or its teachers who become Communists knowing of the purposes of the Party, the Court's judgment overreaches itself in invalidating this Arizona statute. Whether or not Arizona may make knowing membership a crime, it need not retain the member as an employee and is entitled to insist that its employees disclaim, under oath, knowing membership in the designated organizations and to condition future employment upon future abstention from membership. It is, therefore, improper to invalidate the entire statute in this declaratory judgment action. If the imposition of criminal penalties under the present Act is invalid, the Court should so limit its holding and remand the case to the Arizona courts to determine the severability of the criminal provisions under the severability provisions of the Act itself (*Id.* at 23).

2. *Keyishian v. Board of Regents* (N.Y.), 385 U.S. 589, 87 S. Ct. 675 (1967).

Just one year after *Elfbrandt* this case, dealing with virtually the same issue, also reached the United States Supreme Court for final settlement. In essence, it tested the much-litigated Feinberg Law.

In this case teachers were again dismissed for refusal to sign affidavits stating they were not Communists. Although a three-judge federal court held the program, under which the teachers were dismissed, to be constitutional, the United States Supreme Court ruled otherwise.

In its opinion, delivered by Justice Brennan, the High Court held that the provisions of the Feinberg Law barring from employment in public schools any person wilfully advocating or teaching the doctrine of forcible overthrow of the government "are unconstitutionally vague and violate the First Amendment." Pertinent excerpts from the court's opinion follow:

> We do not have the benefit of a judicial gloss by the New York courts enlightening us as to the scope of this complicated plan. In light of the intricate administrative machinery for its enforcement, this is not surprising. The very intricacy of the plan and the uncertainty as to the scope of its proscriptions make it a highly efficient *in terrorem* mechanism. It would be a bold teacher who would not stay as far as possible from utterances or acts which might jeopardize his living by enmeshing him in this intricate machinery (385 U.S. at 601).

There can be no doubt of the legitimacy of New York's interest in protecting its educational system from subversion. But "even though the governmental purpose be legitimate and substantial, that purpose cannot be pursued by means that broadly stifle fundamental personal liberties when the end can be more narrowly achieved" (*Id.* at 602).

Our Nation is deeply committed to safeguarding academic freedom, which is of transcendent value to all of us and not merely to the teachers concerned. That freedom is therefore a special concern of the First Amendment, which does not tolerate laws that cast a pall of orthodoxy over the classroom. "The vigilant protection of constitutional freedoms is nowhere more vital than in the community of American schools." The classroom is peculiarly the "marketplace of ideas." The Nation's future depends upon leaders trained through wide exposure to that robust exchange of ideas which discovers truth "out of a multitude of tongues, [rather] than through any kind of authoritative selection" (*Id.* at 603).

It is noteworthy that the same Justices (Clark, Harlan, Stewart and White) who dissented in the preceding *Elfbrandt* opinion also dissented in this case. Justice Clark wrote for the minority, in the following terms:

It is clear that the Feinberg Law, in which this Court found "no constitutional infirmity" in 1952, has been given its death blow today. Just as the majority here finds that there "can be no doubt of the legitimacy of New York's interest in protecting its education system from subversion" there can also be no doubt that "the be-all and end-all" of New York's effort is here. And, regardless of its correctness, neither New York nor the several States that have followed the teaching of *Adler* ... for some 15 years, can ever put the pieces together again. No court has ever reached out so far to destroy so much with so little (*Id.* at 622).

The majority says the Feinberg Law is bad because it has an "overbroad sweep." I regret to say — and I do so with deference — that the majority has by its broadside swept away one of our most precious rights, namely, the right of self-preservation. Our public educational system is the genius of our democracy. The minds of our youth are developed there and the character of that development will determine the future of our land. Indeed, our very existence depends upon it. The issue here is a very narrow one. It is not freedom of speech, freedom of thought, freedom of press, freedom of assembly or of association, even in the Communist Party. It is simply this: May the State provide that one who, after a hearing with full judicial review, is found to have wilfully and deliberately, advocated, advised, or taught that our Government should be overthrown by force or violence or other unlawful means; or to have wilfully and deliberately printed, published, etc., any book or paper that so advocated *and to have personally* advocated such doctrine himself; or to have wilfully and deliberately become a member of an organization that advocates such doctrine is prima facie disqualified from teaching in its university? My answer, in keeping with all our cases up until today is "Yes"! (*Id.* at 628-29).

§ 5.4 Invoking the Fifth Amendment.

Following enactment of the Feinberg Law, there was a pronounced trend for school employees to invoke the Fifth Amendment by way of refusing to testify before legislative committees investigating subversive affiliation, on the grounds that to do so might incriminate them.

1. *Daniman v. Board of Education of the City of New York,* 202 Misc. 915, 118 N.Y.S.2d 487 (1953).

In this early case, teachers were dismissed for their refusal to answer questions as to their relation to the Communist Party or to Communism. At the advice of their lawyers, the teachers merely stated that they refused to answer lest their answers might incriminate them.

The court, therefore, held "that their answer might tend to incriminate them, they were properly discharged under city charter for refusal to answer such questions."

The court concluded its remarks on the case as follows:

When the officials of these boards, whose duty it is to safeguard all children from being debauched mentally and morally, find that their teachers are putting on this false show of indignation over being exposed as apparent enemies of the nation, and are falsely claiming to be immune to questions that go to the roots of their honesty and loyalty, and that when questioned they will not say yes or no to whether they belong to a group generally regarded as godless, disloyal, destructive and dishonest, are they arbitrary and capricious in dismissing them? Indeed, would not their retention of petitioners be grossly arbitrary and childishly capricious? Is not the cleansing of the city's school system of such foulness and danger one of the "affairs of the City" ... which the respondent boards are in duty bound to attend to? ... These respondents merely had to later carry out the formalities; the Legislature made the petitioners their own executioners (118 N.Y.S.2d at 493-94).

2. *Board of Education of City of Los Angeles v. Wilkinson,* 270 P.2d 82 (Cal. 1954).

In this case the District Court of Appeals held that in view of a rule of the Board of Education requiring a teacher to answer questions of any legislative committee relating to activities in the Communist Party, "refusal of a teacher to answer questions of State Senate Committee concerning his activities in communism constituted unprofessional conduct, authorizing her discharge" (*Id.* at 82).

The court added:

> A teacher's employment in the public schools
> is a privilege, not a right. A condition implicit
> in that privilege is loyalty to the government
> under which the school system functions. It is
> the duty of every teacher to answer proper
> questions in relation to his fitness to teach our
> youth when put to him by a lawfully
> constituted body authorized to propound such
> questions. . . . The power of a teacher to mold
> the thoughts and conduct of children is so
> great that surely the State must have power to
> inquire into the beliefs of the teacher in whose
> care the youth of the country is placed for
> instruction. Such conduct, furthermore, is
> unprofessional under the rule adopted by the
> Board of Education (*Id.* at 85-6).

3. *Kaplan v. School District of Philadelphia,* 388 Pa.
213, 130 A.2d 672 (1957).

This case also involved a teacher whose refusal to
testify resulted in her legal suspension from duty as a
teacher. As in the previous case, the court emphasized
the obligation of the teacher in setting a good example
for the pupils who frequently attempt to emulate their
teachers:

> Children respect and look for guidance to
> their school teacher second only to their
> parents; their immature minds are influenced
> not only by what they are actually taught in
> the classroom but also by the personality of
> their teacher; the impressions they receive in

school are bound to color their adult lives and
to determine for them, as they advance into
manhood and womanhood, whether they
emerge as patriotic or as unfaithful citizens. In
short, it is essential, in order to protect our
children from treacherous influences, that
persons who advocate or participate in
subversive doctrines should not be employed,
or if employed should not be retained, as
teachers in our public schools, and any teacher
dismissed for such a reason cannot properly
claim that any constitutional or legal right is
thereby violated (130 A.2d at 680).

4. *Beilan v. Board of Education* (Pa.), 357 U.S. 399, 78
S. Ct. 1317 (1958).

This case had a different twist on the issue of
invoking the Fifth Amendment, where subversive
leanings of teachers are suspected. Here a public school
teacher was discharged on the ground of
"incompetency" evidenced by the teacher's refusal of
the Superintendent's request to confirm or refute
information as to the teacher's loyalty and his activities
in certain allegedly subversive organizations.

After having consulted with his counsel, Beilan
declined to answer that question or others of that type,
as was his privilege in accordance with the Fifth
Amendment. Since the Pennsylvania statutes did not
have a "catch-all" phrase such as "unbecoming
conduct" as a reason for dismissing teachers, the
dismissal was made on the ground of "incompetency"
as allowed by the Public School Code. The County Court
of Common Pleas set aside Beilan's discharge, holding

that the Board should have followed the procedure specified by the Pennsylvania Loyalty Act. The Supreme Court of Pennsylvania reversed the decision of the Court of Common Pleas whereupon it was appealed to the United States Supreme Court for final settlement.

In a five to four decision, with Justice Burton writing for the majority, the High Court sustained the state Supreme Court, and thereby held that Beilan's discharge did not violate the Due Process Clause of the Fourteenth Amendment.

Justice Burton wrote as follows:

> By engaging in teaching in the public schools, petitioner did not give up his right to freedom of belief, speech or association. He did, however, undertake obligations of frankness, candor and cooperation in answering inquiries made of him by his employing Board examining into his fitness to serve it as a public school teacher (357 U.S. at 405).

> Petitioner's refusal to answer was not based on the remoteness of his 1944 activities. He made it clear that he would not answer any question of the same type as the one asked. Petitioner blocked from the beginning any inquiry into his Communist activities, however relevant to his present loyalty. The Board based its dismissal upon petitioner's refusal to answer any inquiry about his relevant activities — not upon those activities themselves. It took care to charge petitioner

with incompetency, and not disloyalty. It found him insubordinate and lacking in frankness and candor — it made no finding as to his loyalty (*Id.* at 405-6).

Chief Justice Warren, as one of the dissenters, stated:

> I believe the facts of record in No. 63 compel the conclusion that Beilan's plea of the Fifth Amendment before a subcommittee of the House Committee in Un-American Activities was so inextricably involved in the Board's decision to discharge him that the validity of the Board's action cannot be sustained without consideration of this ground. The clearest indication of this is the fact that for 13 months following petitioner's refusal to answer the Superintendent's questions, he was retained as a school teacher and continually rated "satisfactory," yet five days after his appearance before the House subcommittee petitioner was suspended. Since a plea of the Fifth Amendment before a congressional committee is an invalid basis for discharge from public employment, I would reverse the judgment approving petitioner's dismissal (*Id.* at 411).

§ 5.5 Testifying against one's associates.

1. *Board of Education of City of New York v. Allen,* 6 Misc.2d 453, 167 N.Y.S.2d 221 (1956).

Although teachers may be required to answer questions concerning their own affiliation with the Communist Party, they may not, according to this case, be required to disclose the names of other presently-employed teachers known to be or to have been members.

Here the superintendent of schools, under authority delegated to him by the board, suspended certain confessed members who, "Upon the grounds of conscience and moral scruples," refused to disclose names of others. They appealed to the Commissioner of Education, who enjoined the board and superintendent from requiring these teachers to identify those they know to have been members of the Communist Party. On appeal to the court, the Commissioner's decision was upheld.

The rationale of the Commissioner's ruling is stated, in part, as follows:

> The literature of Communists who have recanted specifically sets forth allegations that their ilk have deliberately named persons who have had no connection with the organization for party reasons. Even if a person so named is exonerated by lack of proof or is able to develop sufficient proof to allay suspension, he is marked for life. The instant a name is uttered the public becomes aware of it. A school system which sets one teacher against another in this manner is not conducive toward the strength and cohesion which needs to exist in order to instill character into the student body.

> The respondent board now insists that unless they can require any employee to name any person whom he accuses of being a

Communist they are "thwarted at a vital stage." I am convinced that this is not so. The Courts have quite recently indicated that a board of education cannot convict a teacher of being a Communist unless that board can establish its case after a jury trial. In my judgment the board is most optimistic if it believes that a jury will convict on the flimsy evidence of informers. It is, of course, perhaps true that the board, when the name is known, might be able to obtain corroborating evidence. It is also possible for the board to call the teacher in and ask whether he or she is a Communist. The argument that the board needs someone to name names is of no value here because the board in any event can call in any teacher, or for that matter all teachers and ask if they are Communists (167 N.Y.S.2d at 224).

Chapter 6

GROUNDS FOR TEACHER DISMISSAL

§ 6.1 Statutory provisions for teacher dismissal.

There are various reasons stipulated in the statutes for which teachers may be legally dismissed from their positions. The reasons most frequently mentioned are "immorality," "incompetency" and "insubordination." Other reasons less frequently mentioned are "inefficiency," "neglect of duty" and "unprofessional" or "improper conduct." Some statutes list multiple reasons, such as those listed here, and then to be certain to cover the entire spectrum they may be supplemented by adding the clause "and for other good and just cause."

The responsibility of school boards, as well as those of the courts, would be greatly facilitated if just the catch-all phrase, "for good and just cause," were stipulated in the statute as a legal reason for dismissing a teacher whose continued presence, service or behavior would be detrimental to the school and the students, regardless of which reasons for dismissal are stated in the statute.

Where a statute does not contain a "catch-all" phrase, a specific word may be construed as being that inclusive. For example, the Pennsylvania courts have, on several occasions, applied a broad interpretation to the word "incompetency" which was the only reason for

183

teacher dismissal stipulated in the Pennsylvania statute. An illustrative case is that of *Beilan v. Board of Education, supra,* where a teacher was lawfully dismissed for "incompetency" because he refused to answer questions regarding his alleged affiliation with a subversive organization.

1. *Watts v. Seward School Board,* 395 P.2d 372 (Alaska 1964).

Likewise in this case, a broad interpretation was given to the word "immorality," when two teachers were legally dismissed for "immorality," as defined in the statute, when they solicited a labor union and fellow teachers in an attempt to remove from office the superintendent and members of the school board.

2. *Watts v. Seward School District,* 421 P.2d 586 (Alaska 1966).

In subsequent litigation on the case, the Supreme Court of Alaska noted that the term "immorality," attached to the reason for dismissal of a teacher, could be an "unnecessary stigma" and that, therefore:

> [T]he designation or title of immorality should be removed from the "catch-all" definition of conduct and a designation such as "conduct unbecoming a teacher" be substituted. The definition would then cover immorality in all of its aspects, including all shades of unacceptable social behavior and would continue to serve the useful purpose of a "catch-all" clause which so many states have found to be a necessity in this area of legislation (*Id.* at 591).

§ 6.2 Immorality.

1. *Schuman v. Pickert,* 277 Mich. 225, 269 N.W. 152 (1936).

Since statutes frequently cite "immorality" as a legal reason for teacher dismissal, without defining its meaning, the courts have occasionally attempted to do so. For example, in this early case, the Supreme Court of Michigan commented as follows:

> "Immorality" is not necessarily confined to matters sexual in their nature; it may be that which is contra bonos mores; or not moral, inconsistent with rectitude, purity or good morals; contrary to conscience or moral law; wicked; vicious; licentious, as, an immoral man or deed. Its synonyms are: Corrupt, indecent, depraved, dissolute; and its antonyms are: Decent, upright, good, right. That may be immoral which is not decent (269 N.W. at 152).

2. *Jarvella v. Willoughby-Eastlake City School District,* 12 Ohio Misc. 288, 233 N.E.2d 143 (1967).

The Court of Common Pleas of Ohio also undertook to add meaning to the term, "immorality," in the following manner:

> Whatever else the term "immorality" may mean to many, it is clear that when used in a statute it is inseparable from "conduct." Both counsel agree that this is so. But it is not "immoral conduct" considered in the abstract. It must be considered in the context in which the Legislature considered it, as conduct which is hostile to the welfare of the general public;

185

more specifically in this case, conduct which is hostile to the welfare of the school community (233 N.E.2d at 145).

The actual case concerned the dismissal of a teacher on the grounds of "immorality" for writing letters which allegedly "contain language which many adults would find gross, vulgar and offensive and which some eighteen-year-old males would find unsurprising and fairly routine."

In ruling in favor of the teacher, the court offered the following guidelines for school officials to restrain the conduct of teachers in this area:

> In providing standards to guide school boards in placing restraints on conduct of teachers, the Legislature is concerned with the welfare of the school community. Its objective is the protection of students from corruption. This is a proper exercise of the power of the state to abridge personal liberty and to protect larger interests. But reasonableness must be the governing criterion. The board can only be concerned with "immoral conduct" to the extent that it is, in some way, inimical to the welfare of the school community. The private speech or writings of a teacher, not in any way inimical to that welfare, are absolutely immaterial in the application of such standard (*Id.* at 145).

3. *Morrison v. State Board of Education,* 74 Cal. Rptr. 116 (1969).

Judiciaries disagree as to whether homosexuality constitutes immorality to the extent that it would be just cause for teacher dismissal. For example, in this case a State Board of Education attempted to revoke a teacher's life certificate to teach children because of his admitted homosexual act. A Court of Appeals affirmed the judgment of a lower court that held the teacher's conduct was immoral and unprofessional which authorized revocation of his certificate. On further appeal, however, the Supreme Court of California reversed the judgments of the lower courts and stated its reason for doing so:

> We cannot believe the Legislature intended to compel disciplinary measures against teachers who committed such peccadillos if such passing conduct did not affect students or fellow teachers. Surely incidents of extra-marital heterosexual conduct against a background of years of satisfactory teaching would not constitute "immoral conduct" sufficient to justify revocation of a life diploma without any showing of an adverse effect on fitness to teach (*Id.* at 183).

4. *Burton v. Cascade School District Union High School No. 5,* 353 F. Supp. 254 (Ore. 1973).

The facts of this case indicate that although a teacher confessed she was a homosexual, there was no evidence that she was "derelict in her teaching duties or that she made advances toward any student."

Nevertheless, the Cascade School Board dismissed the teacher and sought support for its action from a state statute which authorized dismissal of teachers for

187

"immorality." Since the statute failed to define immorality, the court held that the statute was too vague as to classify homosexuality as being immoral, and stated:

> This statute vests in the school board the power to dismiss teachers for immorality. However, the statute does not define immorality. Immorality means different things to different people, and its definition depends on the idiosyncracies of the individual school board members. It may be applied so broadly that every teacher in the state could be subject to discipline. The potential for arbitrary and discriminatory enforcement is inherent in such a statute.
>
> A statute so broad makes those charged with the enforcement the arbiters of morality for the entire community. In doing so, it subjects the livelihood of every teacher in the state to the irrationality and irregularity of such judgments. The statute is vague because it fails to give fair warning of what conduct is prohibited and because it permits erratic and prejudicial exercise of authority (*Id.* at 255).

5. *Pettit v. State Board of Education,* 10 Cal. App. 3d 29, 109 Cal. Rptr. 665 (1973).

This case could hardly be classified as one that involved no more than mere "peccadillos." According to the case report, the plaintiff teacher and her husband belonged to "The Swingers Club," devoted primarily to promote diverse school activities between members of the party. Testimony revealed that:

... plaintiff has engaged in acts of sexual intercourse and oral copulation with men other than her husband; that ... although plaintiff's services as a teacher have been "satisfactory," and although she is unlikely to repeat the sexual misconduct, nevertheless she has engaged in immoral and unprofessional conduct, in acts involving moral turpitude, and in acts evidencing her unfitness for service (109 Cal. Rptr. at 667).

On the basis of such findings, the board dismissed the teacher. The Supreme Court of California agreed with the board's action, and stated:

A teacher in the public school system is regarded by the public and pupils in the light of an exemplar, whose words and actions are likely to be followed by the children coming under her care and protection. In the instant case, the board and trial court were entitled to conclude, on the basis of the expert testimony set forth above and the very nature of the misconduct involved, that Mrs. Pettit's illicit and indiscreet actions disclosed her unfitness to teach in public elementary schools (*Id.* at 670).

Despite the above strong statement in the majority opinion there was one dissenting judge who argued as follows:

I submit that the majority opinion is blind to the reality of sexual behavior. Its view that teachers in their private lives should exemplify

189

Victorian principles of sexual morality, and in the classroom should subliminally indoctrinate the pupils in such principles, is hopelessly unrealistic and atavistic. The children of California are entitled to competent and dedicated teachers; when, as in this case, such a teacher is forced to abandon her lifetime profession, the children are the losers (*Id.* at 675).

6. *Board of Education of El Monte School District v. Calderon*, 35 Cal. App. 3d 492, 110 Cal. Rptr. 916 (1974).

A number of cases have been adjudicated, particularly in California, where *oral copulation* has been the subject of litigation. In the instant case a male teacher had been charged with having engaged in an act of oral copulation with another man for which a criminal complaint charged him with violation of a section of the Penal Code.

Although a superior court acquitted the teacher of a criminal charge, the Court of Appeals rejected the lower court decision, and ruled that despite the Penal Code, the Education Code does not preclude the board of education from discharging a teacher for a sex offense. Accordingly the Court of Appeals abided by the findings of the trial court that:

... defendant did engage in the act of oral copulation charged by plaintiff Board; this conduct was indicative of corruption, indecency, depravity, dissoluteness, and shamelessness, showing moral indifference to opinions of respectable members of the community and an inconsiderate attitude toward good order and public welfare ... (110 Cal. Rptr. at 918).

The Court of Appeals agreed with the trial court's contention that "the defendant's conduct is immoral conduct and he is not entitled to recover any back salary." In support of its stand, the court stated:

> We reasonably assume, therefore, that our Legislature properly intended by the enactment of the pertinent sections of the Education Code to permit school boards to shield children of tender years from the possible detrimental influence of teachers who commit acts described therein even though they are not found guilty beyond a reasonable doubt. . . . Finally, the criminal charge between the defendant and the State was penal in nature while the case between defendant and the Board is remedial, for the protection of young children (*Id.* at 920-921).

7. *Tomerlin v. Dade County School Board,* 318 So.2d 159 (Fla. Ct. App. 1975).

Here the Dade County School dismissed Tomerlin, a tenured elementary school teacher, for immoral conduct with his nine-year-old stepdaughter. He appealed to the State Board of Education who sustained the dismissal.

Tomerlin was found guilty of immoral behavior for performing cunnilingus on his stepdaughter. Such action was in conflict with the Florida statute which "regulates the conduct of persons in the teaching profession." In a defense attempt, Tomerlin contended that the statute was unconstitutional because it had no

connection with his job performance. In disregarding
this contention, the court stated:

> Any reasonable person should know that the
> act performed by Tomerlin was immoral, and
> was prohibited by the statute. ... Although
> Tomerlin's immoral act was done at his home
> and after school hours, it was indirectly related
> to his job. His conduct is an incident of a
> perverse personality which makes him a
> danger to school children and unfit to teach
> them. Mothers and fathers would question the
> safety of their children; children would discuss
> Tomerlin's conduct and morals. All of these
> relate to Tomerlin's job performance (*Id.* at
> 160).

8. *Weissman v. Board of Education of Jefferson
County School District,* 547 P.2d 1267 (Colo. 1976).

At the time of this writing this is the most recent case
involving "immorality" as a ground for teacher
dismissal. The case involved a tenured teacher who had
"earned the reputation as an excellent teacher and was
noted for his particularly good rapport with students"
(*Id.* at 1270).

The teacher was assigned to accompany students on
field trips to study different cultures in the Southwest.
It was on one of these trips where the actions of the
teacher prompted litigation involving his immoral
actions which led to his dismissal.

The testimony of one of the adult chaperones declared
that:

During the journey, he engaged in activities with several of the female students in the van, which he characterized as "good-natured horseplay" and which consisted of touching and tickling the girls on various parts of their bodies and occasionally between the legs in proximity to the genital area. There was reciprocal conduct on the part of the girls. During the course of this conduct, the dialogue between appellant and these students was occasionally vulgar, suggestive in nature, and contained many sexual innuendos (*Id.* at 1270).

After the board's action of dismissal for immoral behavior, the appellant argued that the statute pertaining to "immorality" as cause for dismissal was unconstitutional because it was "excessively vague, means different things to different people, and inevitably subjects teachers to the irrational and arbitrary whims of potentially hostile school board members" (*Id.* at 1272).

The appellant further contended that:

"even assuming that he did act immorally, the panel's findings of fact, as adopted by the board, fail to show that his conduct impaired his ability to perform his duties as a teacher, indeed there was no finding that he did not continue to enjoy the admiration and respect of his students and their parents" (*Id.* at 1272).

In holding the appellant teacher guilty of "immorality" as just cause for dismissal the court stated in part:

In determining whether the teacher's conduct indicates an unfitness to teach, the board of education may properly consider such matters as the age and maturity of the teacher's students, the likelihood that his conduct may have adversely affected students and other teachers, the degree of such adversity, the proximity or remoteness in time of the conduct, the likelihood that the conduct may be repeated, the motives underlying it, and the extent to which discipline may have a chilling effect upon either the rights of the teacher involved or other teachers (*Id.* at 1273).

We emphasize that the board's power to dismiss and discipline teachers is not merely punitive in nature and is not intended to permit the exercise of personal moral judgment by board members. Rather, it exists and finds its justification on the state's legitimate interest in protecting the school community from harm, and its exercise can only be justified upon a showing that such harm has or is likely to occur. In view of these considerations and of the desirability of preventing unfit teachers from adversely influencing students, we conclude that the board of education may properly dismiss those teachers whose misbehavior has had the requisite degree of adverse impact (*Id.* at 1273).

§ 6.3 Incompetency.

The term "incompetency" is frequently cited in the school codes as a "catch-all" term for any shortcoming which might befall a teacher. These courts have reasoned that incompetency encompasses and is synonymous with immorality, inefficiency, insubordination, poor teaching, lack of discipline, physical incapacity, mental unfitness, emotional instability, and lack of self control.

1. *Crawfordsville v. Hays,* 42 Ind. 200 (1873).

The rule governing the dismissal of teachers for incompetency has been clearly expressed by the Indiana Supreme Court in this early case:

> A teacher, doubtless, like a lawyer, surgeon, or physician, when he undertakes an employment, impliedly agrees that he will bestow upon that service a reasonable degree of learning, skill, and care. When he accepts an employment as teacher in any given school, he agrees, by implication, that he has the learning necessary to enable him to teach the branches that are to be taught therein, as well as that he has the capacity, in a reasonable degree, of imparting that learning to others. He agrees, also, that he will exercise a reasonable degree of care and diligence in the advancement of his pupils in their studies, in preserving harmony, order, and discipline in the school, and that he will himself conform, as near as may be, to such reasonable rules and regulations as may be established by competent authority for the government of the school. . . .

Now, if a teacher, although he has been
employed for a definite length of time, proves
to be incompetent, and unable to teach the
branches of instruction he has been employed
to teach, either from a lack of learning, or from
an utter want of capacity to impart his learning
to others; or if, in any other respect, he fails to
perform the obligations resting upon him as
such teacher, whether arising from the
express terms of his contract or by necessary
implication, he has broken the agreement on
his part, and the trustees are clearly
authorized to dismiss him from his
employment (*Id.* at 209-10).

2. *Horosko v. Mount Pleasant Township School
District,* 335 Pa. 369, 6 A.2d 866 (1939).

In this oft-quoted case the Supreme Court of
Pennsylvania approved the board's dismissal of a
teacher who "acted as waitress and, on occasion, as
bartender, in husband's beer garden and in presence of
pupils, teacher took a drink of beer, served beer to
customers, and shook dice with customers for drinks,
played and showed customers how to play the pinball
machine, justified dismissal of teacher on grounds of
"incompetency" (6 A.2d at 867).

The Supreme Court, which approved the teacher's
dismissal, was of the opinion that the term
"incompetency" has a common and approved usage, as
indicated by the following excerpt:

The context does not limit the meaning of the
word to lack of substantive knowledge of the
subjects to be taught. Common and approved

usage gives a much wider meaning. For example, with reference to a number of supporting decisions it is defined: "A relative term without technical meaning. It may be employed as meaning disqualification; inability; incapacity; lack of ability, legal qualification, or fitness to discharge the required duty" (*Id.* at 869).

3. *Guthrie v. Board of Education of Jefferson County,* 298 S.W.2d 691 (Ky. 1957).

As indicated by this case, *inability to maintain discipline is commonly considered* as incompetency warranting dismissal. Here a school board discharged a teacher for reasons of "incompetency and inefficiency." Uncontested testimony of school administrators regarding the discharged teacher was as follows:

> Not only was she unable to preserve proper order in the classrooms over which she presided, but she was deficient in controlling pupils placed under her care on the play ground. Her pupils were unhappy and ill at ease, her classroom was full of tension and confusion, with the result that group work and individual incentive were lacking. She was transferred from school to school, five in all, in an effort to adjust her to a general atmosphere in which she could instruct effectively, but such transfers failed to bring about any beneficial results (*Id.* at 692).

4. *Mims v. West Baton Rouge Parish School Board,* 315 So.2d 349 (La. App. 1975).

Despite the fact that a *black* teacher claimed racial discrimination in dismissal charges instituted by a white principal, the court affirmed the board's dismissal of the teacher on the grounds of "incompetency and neglect of duty" which were listed as follows:

1. Failure to follow the policy established for the Devall School faculty relating to reporting absences from school.

2. Failure to turn in to the office, reports and materials as requested in the classroom.

3. Failure to maintain discipline as a conducive learning environment in the classrooms.

4. Failure on the part of the teacher to initiate suggestive recommendations for improvement as presented by supervisors during conferences.

5. Failure to follow the established procedures relating to the maintenance of the student report card and cumulative card.

6. Failure to follow the policy established for the Devall School faculty regarding the daily reporting of the teacher lunch count.

7. Failure on the part of the teacher to report or pay for the exact number of days she actually ate in the lunchroom during the months of March, April, and May, 1971.

8. Failure to recognize the needs of the students she teaches and to group, plan, and teach according to those needs.

9. Failure to do the necessary planning and preparation required of an effective teacher.

10. Failure to exhibit the necessary effort, initiative, imagination, and enthusiasm required of an effective teacher.

11. Failure to display a positive attitude toward educable mentally retarded children.

12. Failure to emphasize the importance of individual responsibility in regard to the care of school property (*Id.* at 350).

With respect to the charge of racial discrimination in the board's dismissal of the teacher, the court stated:

> The record is totally barren of evidence in substantiation of Appellant's charge that Misuraca is prejudiced against blacks and is incompetent to evaluate the ability and competence of black teachers. On the contrary, it is shown that Misuraca is an experienced administrator and that his action in bringing charges against Appellant was prompted by good cause, not bias or prejudice (*Id.* at 353).

5. *Saunders v. Reorganized School District No. 2 of Osage County,* 520 S.W.2d 29 (Mo. 1975).

In this case the Supreme Court of Missouri held that the evidence was sufficient to support the board's finding that the teacher had been guilty of incompetency, inefficiency, and insubordination.

> The charges were in substance: that Saunders had failed and refused to instruct the curriculum as directed; that he had refused to discuss the teaching of the curriculum with his superiors; that he had given the students of a second year class their choice of repeating the

first year material or having the subject taught as he (Saunders) wanted to; that he refused to participate in the preparation of a course outline; that his refusal to return to work was unreasonable, and he was guilty of excessive and unreasonable absence; that he refused to discuss teacher evaluations with his superiors; that he was inefficient as shown by the evaluation reports; that he failed and refused to use the required textbooks in his teachings; that he was thus guilty of incompetency, inefficiency and insubordination in the line of duty (*Id.* at 31).

§ 6.4 Insubordination.

1. *State v. Board of Education of Fairfield,* 252 Ala. 254, 40 So.2d 689 (1949).

A brief and concise definition of the term "insubordination" was offered by the Supreme Court of Alabama in the following statement: "The term 'insubordination' is not defined in the statute, but unquestionably it includes the willful refusal of a teacher to obey the reasonable rules and regulations of his or her employing board of education" (40 So.2d at 695).

2. *State v. Board of Regents of University of Nevada,* 70 Nev. 347, 269 P.2d 265 (1954).

The Supreme Court of Nevada provided a slightly broader judicial concept of the term "insubordination" in the following terms:

From the many definitions found in the cases we may say without greater elaboration that "insubordination" imparts willful disregard of express or implied directions, or such a defiant attitude as to be equivalent thereto. "Rebellious," "mutinous," and "disobedient" are often quoted as definitions or synonyms of "insubordination" (269 P.2d at 276).

3. *Millar v. Joint School District No. 2,* 2 Wis.2d 303, 86 N.W.2d 455 (1957).

A teacher's *refusal to attend a meeting is frequently construed as insubordination.* In this case a teacher was dismissed for refusing to attend a meeting of the school board, the purpose of which was to give the teacher the opportunity to resign. His action was one of defiance as indicated by his statement "that in his own heart and mind he was a good teacher — that he would not resign — that Brownlaw could go to hell" (86 N.W.2d at 457). He also remarked that "he was damned if the school board would lead him around with a ring in his nose." He also referred to the board as "lacking guts," "weak-kneed" and being "yellow bellied" (*Id.* at 459).

Since the teacher had been summoned only for the purpose of resigning and not to defend his demeanor, the judgment of the lower court adverse to the teacher was reversed by the Supreme Court of Wisconsin. A dissenting judge, however, stated: "In my opinion, the refusal to attend the meeting constituted a refusal to accede to a reasonable request by his employer and that is insubordination" (*Id.* at 464).

4. *Gilbertson v. McAlister,* 403 F. Supp. 1 (D. Conn. 1975).

In a much later case, a teacher was legally dismissed for *refusal to attend a meeting* with a school principal to discuss the teacher's distribution of leaflets which were derogatory to the school. For example:

> One leaflet focused on the principal of Weaver High School, Stewart Street, stating, among other things, that Mr. Street (1) imposed a "CIA style reign of terror" at the school, where "cop cars ring the school, bluecoats invade the halls and cafeterias [*sic*] on the slightest pretext, and over 100 students have been illegally suspended or expelled; (2) established a "terrified student body, easily regimented for slave labor"; (3) refused to reinstate an expelled militant student "even after a court ordered him to do so"; and (4) used "military riot-control gas" against demonstrating students when he was principal of a school in Camden, New Jersey, in 1972 (*Id.* at 3).

As a consequence of his distribution of materials which were "sharply critical of certain programs and employees" of the school, the principal

> requested that Ms. Gilbertson report to his office on October 23, 1973. Ms. Gilbertson stated that she would appear only if a witness were permitted to accompany her. Thereupon, Mr. Street ordered her to attend the meeting with him, stating that, after they had an initial conference, he would allow her to call in a witness. When she again refused to come to his office, Mr. Street informed her that he considered her refusal to be an act of

insubordination. Despite this warning Ms. Gilbertson failed to appear at Mr. Street's office (*Id.* at 4).

The court held that (1) considered either individually or collectively, the proven charges against plaintiff, including insubordination when she refused to comply with lawful orders of the principal to report to his office, were sufficient to justify her termination as a teacher ... (*Id.* at 1).

5. *Beverlin v. Board of Education of Lewis County,* 216 S.E.2d 554 (W. Va. 1975).

Excessive *absence from teaching duties* is sometimes considered insubordination and cause for teacher dismissal. Of course the extent of the absence is a controlling factor. This case indicates *reasonable* absence is not a ground for dismissal.

Here a teacher was dismissed for *insubordination* because of absence on the first day of school which occurred when the teacher, without permission, absented himself, in order to register for an evening class at the University. The Supreme Court of Appeals of West Virginia ruled against the board's action and supported the decision in the following terms:

> Mr. Beverlin's actions did not support a finding of insubordination and wilful neglect of duty. Although he missed the better part of one school day, his pupils did not suffer his absence, because they were not scheduled to attend classes until later. Moreover, the reason for his absence was to augment his skills with graduate work ... when he became aware of

the conflict with school opening, he made several unsuccessful attempts to notify his principal and assistant principal (*Id.* at 558).

The court agreed the absence was an error, but that the teacher "should have checked on the possibility of late registration or made certain that the principal knew of his whereabouts," and concluded that:

> Therefore, we find that the decisions of Superintendent Brown and the Lewis County Board of Education were arbitrary, and capricious on the basis of the record before us ... (*Id.* at 559).

In a dissenting opinion Judge Neely stated his position as follows:

> I must respectfully dissent from the Court's opinion upon the grounds that I do not believe that the courts, in general, are the repositories of all wisdom. . . .
>
> The majority's opinion is yet one more example of the increasing tendency of courts to undermine the ability of those charged with responsibility to discharge their duties in a competent manner. The increasing substitution of court judgment for the judgments of all other decision-makers causes administration to become increasingly chaotic because of paralysis prompted by a surplusage of procedural and substantive due process which leads not to justice but to total incompetence and inability to govern (*Id.* at 559).

6. *Fernald v. City of Ellsworth Superintending School Committee,* 342 A.2d 704 (Sup. Jud. Ct. of Me. 1975).

In a more flagrant case of absentness a teacher's dismissal was upheld by the Supreme Judicial Court of Maine because the plaintiff's "absence from school duties for two days a month after her plans to be absent had been expressly disapproved by school authorities" (*Id.* at 704).

In support of its decision the court made the following declaration:

> Plaintiff's conduct in the instant case partakes of two separate and distinct elements: First, unauthorized absence from school duties for two days; secondly, an attitude of persistent, willful defiance which amounts to insubordination.... We lay special emphasis on the persistence of plaintiff's willfulness over the course of a month when she made no effort to accommodate herself or even to discuss her needs, as she understood them, with the school administrators.... In short, we are not dealing here with a teacher's ephemeral bad mood, minor clerical omission, or arguable negligence or inattention concerning an incidental matter. Rather, plaintiff's conduct has the marks of a persistent, sustained, and unreasonable course of defiance. Such an attitude, over a course of time, breeches harmonious relations among colleagues and administrators. We think the defendant School Committee was entitled to

conclude that plaintiff's usefulness in the school had become impaired and that the good of the school required her dismissal (*Id.* at 708).

§ 6.5 Grooming violations.

1. *Finot v. Pasadena City Board of Education,* 58 Cal. Rptr. 520 (1967).

Violation of grooming regulations has been the cause for teacher dismissal and litigation. In the instant case the school board dismissed a teacher from his regular teaching assignment because he wore a beard in violation of administrative policy. In support of the policy and ensuing action, school authorities testified that:

> the wearing of beards by male students had been a continuous problem at John Muir High School ... the appearance of teachers had a definite effect on student dress by way of example and in turn student dress had a definite correlation with student behavior — that is, the well-dressed student generally behaved equally well. Their concern was that appellant's beard might attract undue student attention and thereby interfere with the process of educating them and, more specifically, would make the prohibition against male students wearing beards more difficult to enforce (*Id.* at 522).

> Finot responded by claiming that "his transfer from classroom to home teaching by respondents, because he insisted on wearing a beard while teaching as unconstitutional action

... that depriving him of this right without a valid reason or interest therefor and in the manner in which it was done, was a denial to him of his constitutional guarantees against deprivation of his life, liberty or property without due process of law and the equal protection of the laws (*Id.* at 523).

In holding for the teacher the court stated, in part:

A beard, for a man, is an expression of his personality. On the one hand it has been interpreted as a symbol of masculinity, of authority and of wisdom. On the other hand it has been interpreted as a symbol of non-conformity and rebellion. But symbols, under appropriate circumstances, merit constitutional protection ... his constitutional right to do so outweighs the *a priori* judgment of the principal and superintendent, however experienced, expert and professional such judgment may have been. Prior restraints of expression may not ordinarily be used to limit 1st Amendment freedoms (*Id.* at 528-29).

2. *Braxton v. Board of Public Instruction of Duval County, Florida,* 303 F. Supp. 958 (M.D. 1969).

In this case the plaintiff teacher claimed that the school committee failed to reappoint him solely because he refused to shave his goatee. Evidence established that the plaintiff was a "superior" French teacher, and the only black teacher on the 110-member faculty of the high school. No evidence, however, was introduced by the defendant school committee to indicate that the wearing of the goatee tended to disrupt discipline or encourage inappropriate dress by students.

In holding for the goateed teacher the court declared:

> In reaching this conclusion, the Court does not treat lightly the problems of discipline and deportment of students or discourage reasonable regulations designed to insure appropriate dress for students. No evidence has been presented, however, which would indicate that the wearing of a goatee by Mr. Peak might reasonably be expected to cause a disruption of the Ribault Senior High School or to encourage inappropriate dress by students. Nor was there any evidence that any such disruption in fact occurred.
>
> The wearing of a beard by a teacher has been held to be a constitutionally protected liberty under the due process clause of the Fourteenth Amendment to the Constitution of the United States, and the wearer of the goatee here involved deserves no less protection; furthermore where, as here, it is worn as "an appropriate expression of his heritage, culture and social pride as a black man" its wearer also enjoys the protection of First Amendment rights, at least the "peripheral protection" referred to in *Finot, supra* (*Id.* at 959).

3. *Ball v. Kerrville Independent School District,* 529 S.W.2d 792 (Tex. Civ. App. 1975).

Despite the present social adjustment to tonsorial styles which were uncommon a decade ago, litigation on the issue continues. The case report here reveals the appellant teacher (Ball) appeared at a general faculty meeting wearing a Vandyke style beard. The District's superintendent believed the beard would be disruptive of the educational process in the school and directed Ball to shave the beard before commencing to teach his classes on September 2nd. Ball did not believe the beard would be disruptive and said he would shave the beard only if it proved disruptive after a trial period. Ball appeared for his classes on September 2nd with the beard and was suspended by the superintendent. On September 3rd, the District Board of Trustees, at a specially called meeting, voted 6-0 to terminate Ball's teaching contract because of his failure to comply with the superintendent's directive (*Id.* at 792-3).

Substantial evidence supported decision of state board of education that trustees of school district had wrongfully terminated teacher's contract for his refusal to shave off his beard as ordered by superintendent who contended that the beard would disrupt education process of the school system (*Id.* at 792).

4. *Hander v. San Jacinto Junior College,* 519 F.2d 273 (C.A. Tex. 1975).

In this case the teacher who wore a beard was informed that his wearing a beard violated the school's newly enacted policy, "The Board gave Hander four days in which to shave his beard or be discharged. He refused to comply and was immediately dismissed ..." (*Id.* at 275).

The court held:

> School authorities may regulate teachers' appearance and activities only when the regulation has some relevance to legitimate administrative or educational functions. . . . In this case, the college contends that the wearing of a beard diminishes the respect which a teacher must have from his students and "the community" in order to properly perform his duties. The college, however, presented no evidence whatsoever to support this position, other than to suggest that the Board of Regents somehow determined that a clean shaven appearance by faculty members was necessary . . . it is illogical to conclude that a teacher's bearded appearance would jeopardize his reputation or pedagogical effectiveness with college students, particularly in view of our *Lansdale* decision which guarantees those students the right to wear their hair and beards in any style they choose.
>
> In view of these considerations, the district court correctly concluded that Hander's discharge was constitutionally impermissible (*Id.* at 277).

5. *James v. Board of Education of Central District No. 1,* 385 F. Supp. 209 (D.C.N.Y. 1974).

In this case it was held that school officials in discharging a teacher violated the constitutional rights of the teacher because he wore a black armband to school as a symbolic protest against the Vietnam War.

When James wore the armband to classes he was asked by the principal (Pillard) why he was wearing the armband.

> James responded: "Because I am against killing." Pillard then told James that he considered the armband a political act against the President of the United States and asked James to take it off. . . . Pillard then sent James to the office of the District Principal, Edward J. Brown, who also asked James why he was wearing the armband. James told Brown that it was to demonstrate his opposition to killing and explained to him the Quaker Meeting and the background of his wearing the armband. Brown told James that he felt that the wearing of the armband had political connotations and that it was "contrary to the teachers' code of ethics, felt it would be disruptive to the education process, and it might lead to further disruptiveness and divisiveness among teachers" (*Id.* at 212).

The court held that the wearing of a black armband, as in *Tinker,* was a first amendment right akin to "pure speech."

The court added:

> Any limitation on the exercise of constitutional rights can be justified only by a conclusion, based upon reasonable inferences flowing from concrete facts and not abstractions, that the interests of discipline or sound education are *materially and*

substantially jeopardized, whether the danger stems initially from the conduct of students or teachers. Although it is not unreasonable to assume that the views of a teacher occupying a position of authority may carry more influence with a student than would those of students *inter sese,* that assumption merely weighs upon the inferences which may be drawn. It does not relieve the school of the necessity to show a reasonable basis for its regulatory policies (*Id.* at 215).

6. *East Hartford Education Association v. Board of Education,* 405 F. Supp. 94 (D. Conn. 1975).

Although the courts generally uphold teachers who violate school regulations prohibiting the wearing of whiskers, goatees, or flamboyant hairstyles, they are more likely to uphold a school's dress code prohibiting the wearing of unconventional clothing. A 1975 federal court case dealing with the issue is illustrative.

Here a United States District Court upheld a dress code which required men teachers to wear jacket, shirt and tie during classroom activity. The plaintiff teacher who violated the regulation stated the following reasons for his choice to wear a sport shirt without a tie or a sport coat or sweater:

(1) that he wishes to present himself to his students as a person not tied to establishment conformity; (2) he wants to symbolically indicate to his students, his association with what he believes to be the ideas of the generation to which the students belong, including the rejection of many of the customs

and values and social outlook of the older generation; and (3) he believes that dress of this type enables him to achieve a closer rapport with his students and thus enhance his ability to teach (*Id.* at 95).

The plaintiffs further claim that any teacher has the constitutional right to dress and conduct himself as his own conscience commands, as long as the manner of dress and conduct do not interfere with any legitimate state interest. They assert that the municipality or the state has no more lawful interest in an unoffensive manner of attire, than it does in the bridal chamber. It is their contention that there has been no showing that the exercise of the forbidden right would materially or substantially interfere with the requirements of appropriate discipline for the proper administration of the school (*Id.* at 96).

The court's response to such arguments is stated, in part, as follows:

It almost goes without saying that parents, as well as a majority of the teaching profession, expect teachers to possess and maintain certain qualities; to have knowledge of their subject and the ability to convey it, to be morally above reproach and to be physically clean, neat and well-groomed. Teachers set an example in dress and grooming for their students to follow. A teacher who understands this precept and adheres to it enlarges the importance of the task of teaching, presents an image of dignity and encourages respect for authority, which acts as a positive factor in maintaining classroom discipline. Most teachers recognize this aspect of their responsibilities, and maintain a standard of good grooming without requiring school boards to adopt rules. Without such regulations, however, some school systems have been faced with male teachers arriving in the classroom wearing "Bermuda shorts" or similarly inappropriate forms of flamboyant dress (*Id.* at 98).

If plaintiff Brimley does not wish to observe the Board's rule, he is free to go elsewhere and find a school system where conformance to a dress code is not required. His freedom of choice in this respect is unlimited. The Court finds that the local Board rule does not violate due process of law under the Fourteenth Amendment, and is not the type of symbolic act that is contemplated to be within the free speech clause of the First Amendment (*Id.* at 99).

Chapter 7

TEACHERS' RIGHTS OUTSIDE THE CLASSROOM

§ 7.1 Engaging in political campaigns.

1. *Board of Education for Logan County v. Akers,* 243 Ky. 177, 47 S.W.2d 1046 (1932).

Although teachers, like all other citizens, have the right to campaign for a candidate, the teachers' rights have their limitations. However, in this case, a school board's policy "that no school teacher who participated in such elections by actively and openly supporting a candidate should be eligible for the position of school teacher in the county," stretched the limitations too far. In striking down the board's rule, the court declared:

> ... there is no showing that Miss Akers did anything that was wrong or corrupt or anything else but what any good citizen has a right to do in the support of the candidate of his choice. This being true, the county board has no right to adopt a rule that would preclude a school teacher from securing a position in the schools because of such support of a subdistrict trustee (47 S.W.2d at 1647).

2. *Goldsmith v. Board of Education of Sacramento,* 66 Cal. 157, 225 Pac. 783 (1924).

This case indicates that it is not so much the words of the teacher that count as the place where they are uttered. The courts frown upon a teacher's influential comments upon controversial political matters before students who constitute a "captive audience." For example, a teacher was charged with making the following campaign statement before his class:

> Many of you know Mr. Golway, what a fine man he is, and that his hopes are to be elected soon. I think he would be more helpful to our department than a lady, and we need more men in our schools. Sometimes your parents do not know one candidate from another; so they might be glad to be informed (225 P. at 783-84).

Consequently the teacher was suspended, on the ground of unprofessional conduct. The court upheld the teacher's suspension and supported its ruling with the concluding statement which follows:

> . . . it is to be observed that the advocacy before the scholars of a public school by a teacher of the election of a particular candidate for a public office in the attempt thus to influence support of such candidate by the pupils and through them by their parents, introduces into the school questions wholly foreign to its purposes and objects. Such conduct certainly is in contravention not only of the spirit of the laws governing the public school system, but of that essential policy according to which the public school system should be maintained in order that it may subserve in the highest degree its purposes (*Id.* at 789).

§ 7.2 Holding public office.

1. *Monaghan v. School District No. 1*, 211 Ore. 360, 315 P.2d 797 (1957).

Although a large majority of the states allow teachers to *serve in the legislature* without forfeiting their tenure, that right may be restricted by constitutional or statutory provisions. For example, the constitution of Oregon:

> creates three distinct and separate departments — the legislature, the executive, and the judicial. This separation is not merely a matter of convenience of governmental mechanism. Its object is basic and vital ... namely, to preclude a commingling of these essentially different powers of government in the same hands (315 P.2d at 800).

In the instant case a teacher contested the applicability of the constitutional provision because, as a teacher, he performed no "official duties" in connection with the school. However, the court concluded that the teacher nevertheless was performing "functions" of the executive department as a teacher and "official duties" of the legislative department, which was contrary to the constitutional provision and therefore illegal.

Therefore, in denying the teacher the right to serve as a state legislator while holding a position as a public school teacher, the Supreme Court of Oregon reasoned as follows:

> There is no suggestion made here that Mr. Monaghan has by reason of his dual positions

217

as legislator and a teacher, used either to the detriment of either department of government, the legislative or executive, nor do we impute to him any unworthy motive in his desire to retain both places at the same time. Our concern is not with what has been done but rather with what might be done, directly or indirectly, if one person is permitted to serve two different departments at the same time. The constitutional prohibition is designed to avoid the opportunities for abuse arising out of such dual service whether it exists or not (*Id.* at 805).

2. *Begich v. Jefferson*, 441 P.2d 27 (Alaska, 1968).

Again, the principle of separation of powers among the separate branches of government was litigated in Alaska where a superintendent and two teachers were serving as legislators while holding their professional positions. The Supreme Court held that they could not hold both positions because the Alaska constitution provides that "no legislator may hold any other office or position of profit under United States or state."

The decision of the Superior Court was affirmed by the Supreme Court of Alaska which concluded:

Alaska's constitutional prohibition against members of our three separate branches of state government holding any other positions of profit under the State of Alaska reflects the intent to guard against conflicts of interest, self-aggrandizement, concentration of power, and dilution of separation of powers in regard to the exercise by these governmental officials of the executive, judicial, and legislative functions of our state government. The rationale underlying such prohibitions can be attributed to the desire to encourage and preserve independence and integrity of action and decision on the part of individual members of our state government. On the other hand, we recognize that citizens should be interested in and seek public office. Public service and concern for the welfare of our citizenry is essential if we are to have a viable state government. By today's decision we have not ruled upon the question of whether article II, section 5's prohibition precludes legislators from holding teaching positions under political subdivisions of the State of Alaska (*Id.* at 35).

3. *Amador v. New Mexico State Board of Education,* 80 N.M. 336, 455 P.2d 840 (1969).

The issue of "dual office holding" was litigated in New Mexico when the State Board of Education adopted a resolution requiring the suspension of the teaching certificate of a teacher elected to the State Board. Upon being served with an order to show cause why his certificate should not be suspended, the teacher sought and was granted an injunction restraining and enjoining the State Board of Education from enforcing its resolution or suspending his teaching certificate.

In holding for the teacher, the Supreme Court of New Mexico stated:

219

... In our view, the suspension of a teacher for incompatibility with membership on the State Board of Education does not fall within the purpose of insuring a high quality of public instruction. Indeed, appellant does not argue that the supposed incompatibility affects teaching performance.... The State Board only has jurisdiction over a school teacher in the instance where the teacher appeals to that Board from an adverse ruling by the local board of education ... (455 P.2d at 842).

4. *Corsall v. Gover,* 10 Misc. 2d 664, 174 N.Y.S.2d 62 (1958).

While it is a well-recognized legal principle that one may not serve as a *local school board member* while holding a "public office" at the same time (see *Edwards v. Board of Education of Yancey County,* 235 N.C. 345, 70 S.E.2d 170 1952), that principle does not apply to a *teacher* holding a public office at the same time. The reason, of course, is that a school board member is a public *officer* whereas a teacher is regarded by the courts to be a public *employee.*

In the instant case, the school board of Oswego discharged and refused to pay the salary of a teacher who accepted a position as a mayor. The school board contended that the position of teacher and office of mayor were incompatible, and by assuming the mayorship, the petitioner vacated his position as a teacher.

The case was complicated by the fact that by virtue of his office as mayor, he was authorized to appoint members of the board of education (with whom he was involved in litigation). Nevertheless, the court ruled that:

> In the case at Bar, the duties of the Mayor of the City and those of a teacher in the City's Public School System are quite independent of each other. In their relations they do not conflict, so that, in the performance of all the duties thereof respectively required by the same person, there is no inconsistency. The position of teacher is not subordinate to, and inconsistent with, that of Mayor, so that, per se, each would interfere with the other. The element of contrariety and antagonism in the discharge of the duties of both offices enters into all such cases as an important element and factor. It can hardly be said that there is any antagonism or contrariety between the positions of teacher and the office of Mayor (174 N.Y.S.2d at 65).

§ 7.3 Expressing opinions on public issues.

1. *Pickering v. Board of Education* (Ill.), 391 U.S. 563, 88 S. Ct. 1731 (1968).

The issue in this significant case was whether public school teachers have the constitutional right to express themselves on matters which are of public concern. The teacher, involved in the case, was dismissed by the board of education for making comments, which were published in the local newspaper, criticizing the board of education and the superintendent of schools for their proposals to raise new revenue. An excerpt from the published letter states:

As I see it, the bond issue is a fight between the Board of Education that is trying to push tax-supported athletics down our throats with education, and a public that has mixed emotions about both of these items because they feel they are already paying enough taxing and simply don't know whom to trust with any more tax money.

I must sign this letter as a citizen, taxpayer and voter, not as a teacher, since that freedom has been taken from the teachers by the administration. Do you really know what goes on behind those stone walls at the high school? (341 U.S. at 578).

The case finally reached the United States Supreme Court where it was held that the dismissal of the teacher was *unconstitutional* because of violating a teacher's right of free speech as guaranteed by the First Amendment.

Although the rationale of the court's ruling is expressed in considerable length, only a brief excerpt is quoted here:

. . . the question whether a school system requires additional funds is a matter of legitimate public concern in which the judgment of the school administration, including the School Board, cannot, in a society that leaves such questions to popular vote, be taken as conclusive. On such a question free and open debate is vital to informed decision-making by the electorate. Teachers are, as a class, the members of a community most likely to have informal and definite opinions as to how funds allotted to the operation of the school should be spent. Accordingly, it is essential that they be able to speak out freely on such questions without fear of retaliatory dismissal (*Id.* at 571-72).

In sum, we hold that, in a case such as this, absent proof of false statements knowingly or recklessly made by him, a teacher's exercise of his right to speak on issues of public importance may not furnish the basis for his dismissal from public employment . . . (*Id.* at 574-75).

2. *Los Angeles Teachers Union v. Los Angeles City Board of Education*, 78 Cal. Rptr. 723 (1969).

The right for public school teachers to exercise their constitutional right of free expression in matters of public concern is generally held legal when done outside the classroom and during off-duty hours. For example, in this case, adjudicated just one year after *Pickering*, a board regulation prohibiting teachers from circulating petitions concerning disputed budget proposals during off-duty hours was struck down by the Supreme Court of California. It may be noted that the language used by the California court significantly resembled that of the United States Supreme Court in *Pickering*:

Teachers, like others, have the right to speak freely and effectively on public questions. . . . The government has no valid interest in restricting or prohibiting speech or speech-related activity simply in order to avert the sort of disturbance, argument or unrest which is inevitably generated by the expression of ideas which are controversial and invite dispute. The danger justifying restriction or prohibition must be one which rises above public inconvenience, annoyance, or unrest. This is so because the free expression of ideas concerning controversial matters is essential to our system of government (*Id.* at 727-28).

3. *Lusk v. Estes*, 361 F. Supp. 653 (U.S.D.C.N.D. Texas 1973).

Lusk, the plaintiff in this case, was denied a renewal of his teaching contract because of his critical utterances concerning alleged deficiences in the school's administration.

At a meeting between the Dallas City councilmen and his constituents Lusk stated that:

"Our schools are breeding grounds for crime" and that there was a need for stricter enforcement of truancy laws. Lusk added, "This is not just a problem of the schools. The city needs to be concerned" (*Id.* at 656).

In upholding the teacher's right to express his opinions on public school matters, such as those indicated above, and others, the court stated:

It can no longer be seriously asserted that teachers have no right to criticize their employers. ... *Pickering* made it clear that a teacher's employment may not be conditional upon the surrender of his constitutional rights. A citizen's right to engage in protected expression is substantially unaffected by the fact that he is also a teacher and, as a general rule, he cannot be deprived of his teaching position merely because he exercises these rights. This rule has been adopted so that the threat of termination of employment may not be used to inhibit the propensity of a teacher to exercise his constitutional rights of freedom of speech and association.

Because of his position in the educational system, a teacher is able to make a significant contribution to the public debate concerning the quality of education in the school in which he teaches. School authorities must nurture and protect, not extinguish and inhibit, the teacher's right to express ideas. Only if the exercise of these rights by the teacher materially and substantially impedes the teacher's proper performance of his daily duties in the classroom or disrupts the regular operation of the school will a restriction of his rights be tolerated (*Id.* at 660).

§ 7.4 Refusing non-classroom assignments.

1. *Parrish v. Moss*, 106 N.Y.S.2d 577 (1951).

This is the first case on the issue of refusing to perform non-classroom assignments, without extra compensation, which created national interest. It arose in the City of New York where the Board of Education made the following regulation:

(1) Every teacher is required to give service outside of regular classroom instruction in the

performance of functions which are essential duties of every teacher.

(2) There is an area of teacher service which is important to the well rounded educational program of the students, but in which teachers participate in varied ways according to their interests, capabilities and school programs. The principal has the responsibility and duty to see that these activities are carried on. The principal may assign a teacher to reasonable amounts of such service beyond the specified hours of classroom instruction, and the teacher is required to render such service.

(3) In the assignment of teachers to these activities, principals are directed to see to it that insofar as is practicable, such assignments are equitably distributed (*Id.* at 580).

The main reason for teachers challenging the legality of the resolutions was that "they unlawfully delegate to the individual principals of the schools the power to fix the duties and hours of the teachers without providing for adequate protection of the teachers" (*Id.* at 581).

In disregarding the argument of the plaintiff teachers, the court upheld the validity of the board resolutions and, at the same time, set forth the following guidelines as to what constitutes reasonable assignments of extra duties:

Any teacher may be expected to take over a study hall; a teacher engaged in instruction in a given area may be expected to devote part of his day to student meetings where supervision of such teacher is, in the opinion of the board, educationally desirable. Teachers in the fields of English and Social Studies and undoubtedly in other areas may be expected to coach plays; physical training teachers may be required to coach both intramural and inter-school athletic teams; teachers may be assigned to supervise educational trips which are properly part of the school curriculum.... The board may not impose upon a teacher a duty foreign to the field of instruction for which he is licensed or employed. A board may not, for instance, require a *mathematics* teacher to coach intramural teams (*Id.* at 584-85).

2. *McGrath v. Burkhard*, 131 Cal. App. 2d 376, 280 P.2d 864 (1955).

Like many of the other cases involving assignments of extra duties for teachers, this case also falls into the area of extracurricular activities. Here certain male teachers rebelled to attend and supervise student behavior at certain non-classroom activities such as football and basketball, the duties of which were described by school authorities as

maintaining order in the school sections of the stands, sitting in the student sections of the stands, reporting disturbances to the police, preventing spectators from going to the playing field, clearing the way for band and drill teams ... preventing smoking in the gymnasium (*Id.* at 866).

The teacher initiating this case had not objected to performing such duties during the probationary period but did so immediately after attaining "permanent" tenure. He then claimed that "the required duties were unreasonable and not within the scope of teaching duties." The court refused to be swayed by such claims, and declared:

> Supervising the students and being present to protect their welfare at school athletic and social activities, conducted under the name and auspices of the school, is within the scope of the contract and such assignments are proper so long as they are distributed impartially (*Id.* at 870).

> We believe that the presence of teachers at such contests should be helpful not only to the students but should be of benefit to the teachers themselves. We believe that the school authorities had the right to determine that such duties should be performed by the teachers assigned thereto. . . . We must presume that the school authorities were acting for what they considered the best interest of the students and the people of the district (*Id.* at 871).

3. *Todd Coronway v. Landsdowne School District No. 785* (Ct. Com. Pl. of Delaware Co. Pa. 1951).

More *menial* assignments than that of supervising behavior at athletic contests may not be judicially condoned. For example, in this case an English teacher sought and was granted a preliminary injunction to restrain school officials from compelling him to *take tickets at a football game.*

228

In considering the case, the court did acknowledge its favor for limited assignments of non-classroom duties, as indicated by the following statement:

> Modern day schools are more and more offering to their students opportunities to participate in extra-curricular activities, most, if not all, of which broaden the experience and knowledge of the pupils participating therein. The assignment of teachers to supervise such activities is well within the powers of the school boards.

The court then made a turn-about in its stand by supplementing the opening comment with these words:

> However, we cannot see how an assignment to collect tickets at a football game can be considered in such a category. Were the petitioners assigned to sit with the students in a cheering section to help to inculcate in them the attributes of loyalty and good sportsmanship, we might regard such an assignment as having some direct relation to the education of his pupils but the assignment to sit beside a gate and collect tickets bears no such relation. It is a task which any adult could perform and can be motivated by the desire of the school board to cut down the expenses of the game. We feel that such an assignment is not within the field which a teacher must perform and to require him to do so is a demotion in type of position.

4. *Pease v. Millcreek Township School District*, 412 Pa. 378, 195 A.2d 104 (1963).

This case confirms the legal principle that school authorities are limited in assigning teachers to non-classroom activities which bear no relation to the purposes for which they are employed. Here a social studies teacher was assigned to supervise a boy's bowling club which met once a week away from school at a local bowling center.

The plaintiff teacher informed the school authorities that he would not accept the non-classroom duty, because "it was beneath his dignity and not appropriate to a teacher." Following a legal hearing the board dismissed the teacher "on the grounds of incompetency, persistent negligence and persistent and willful violation of school laws."

The real crux of the controversy was whether the bowling activity to which Pease was assigned by the board was *so related to the school program* as to justify the board in making the assignment. The court concluded that it was not, and opined that:

> School teachers must realize that they are subject to assignment by the school board to any activity directly related to the school program; classroom duties in school hours do not constitute *all* their duties. On the other hand, school boards must realize that their power of assignment of school teachers to extracurricular duties is not without limitation and restriction; the activity to which a school teacher is assigned must be related to the school program and the assignment must be fairly and reasonably made (195 A.2d at 108).

5. *District 300 Education Association v. Board of Education*, 31 Ill. App. 3d 550, 334 N.E.2d 165 (1975).

In the latest case on this issue, reported at the time of this writing, teachers *unsuccessfully* sought declaratory and injunctive relief against an assignment to perform extracurricular activities. The plaintiff teachers based their suit on an alleged violation of a statute which stated: "A teacher shall not be required to teach on Saturdays or legal school holidays ..." (334 N.E.2d at 166).

In their complaint the teachers referred to instances such as the following: (1) An Industrial Arts teacher was assigned to ride a "Pep" bus on a Saturday; (2) A Mathematics teacher was assigned to supervise an afternoon football game on a Saturday; (3) A Mathematics teacher was assigned to supervise wrestling matches on two different Saturdays; (4) A Biology teacher was assigned to supervise a basketball game on a Saturday night.

The Board of Education defended its case by stating:

> This section, it will be noted, refers only to *teaching* at such times and is not concerned with the supervising or chaperoning duties set out in the plaintiffs' complaint. The gist of the complaint is that such assignments as indicated above bear no reasonable relationship to the contractual duties imposed on the plaintiffs under their teaching contracts (*Id.* at 166-67).

231

After referring to the case of *Parrish v. Moss, supra* the court stated:

"The broad grant of authority to fix duties of teachers is not restricted to classroom instruction. Any teaching duty within the scope of the license held by a teacher may properly be imposed. The day in which the concept was held that teaching duty was limited to classroom instruction has long since been passed. Children are being trained for citizenship and the inspiration and leadership in such training is the teacher." Supervision at football or basketball games or at musical programs is certainly not to be equated with janitor or police service and we find the case of *Parrish v. Moss* on the whole rather an authority for the defendants than for the plaintiffs on the question of extracurricular duties (*Id.* at 168).

The assignments objected to do not appear to have been onerous in nature or unreasonably time consuming. They are not demeaning to the professional stature of the teacher and there is no evidence that such assignments were made in a discriminatory manner ... (*Id.* at 168).

The duties assigned to the plaintiffs were necessary adjuncts to normal school activities and were neither demeaning in character nor unreasonably burdensome. We think they were within the discretion of the school authorities to require as part of the teachers' duties (*Id.* at 168).

Chapter 8

RIGHT TO STRIKE

§ 8.1   Judicial reaction to teacher strikes.
§ 8.2   Judicial view on sanctions.
§ 8.3   Imposition of penalties.
§ 8.4   Right to picket.

§ 8.1 Judicial reaction to teacher strikes.

1. *Norwalk Teachers Association v. Board of Education*, 138 Conn. 269, 83 A.2d 482 (1951).

For many years the vexing question regarding the teachers' right to strike had never been been actually litigated. In 1951, however, a prominent and precedential case on the issue was adjudicated in Connecticut. Here a teachers' strike had hardly begun before both the teachers and the school board became so concerned as to what the legal consequences of a sustained strike might be that they sought and obtained a *declaratory judgment* from the court, to determine the respective legal rights and liabilities of the parties involved. The declaratory judgment of the court follows:

> It should be the aim of every employee of the government to do his or her part to make it function as efficiently and economically as possible. The drastic remedy of the organized strike to enforce the demands of the unions of government employees is in direct contravention of this principle (93 A.2d at 484).

After citing a number of former cases where the right of governmental employees to strike was litigated the court declared as follows:

Few cases involving the right of unions of government employees to strike to enforce their demands have reached courts of last resort. That right has usually been tested by an application for an injunction forbidding the strike. The right of the governmental body to this relief has been uniformly upheld. It has been put on various grounds: public policy; interference with governmental function; illegal discrimination against the right of any citizen to apply for government employment (when the union sought a closed shop). The following cases do not necessarily turn on the specific right to strike, but the reasoning indicates that, if faced with that question, the court would be compelled to deny that right to public employees (*Id.* at 484-85).

2. *Wichita Public Schools Employees Union v. Smith,* 194 Kan. 2, 397 P.2d 357 (1964).

The judicial view expressed in *Norwalk* was solidified in a later case, where the Supreme Court of Kansas ruled that:

The objects of a political subdivision are governmental — not commercial. It is created for public purposes and has none of the peculiar characteristics of enterprises maintained for private gain. It has no authority to enter into negotiations with labor unions concerning wages and make such negotiations the basis for final appropriations. Strikes against a political subdivision to enforce collective bargaining would in effect amount to strikes against the government.

It appears to be a uniform rule that the wages, hours and working conditions of governmental employees are to be fixed by statutes, ordinances or regulations and that state laws which in general terms secure the rights to employees to enter into collective bargaining agreements with respect to such matters are not intended to apply to public employees ... (397 P.2d at 360).

3. *Anderson Federation of Teachers v. School City of Anderson*, 251 N.E.2d 15 (Ind. 1969).

Also the Supreme Court of Indiana upheld a superior court which adjudged a teacher's union in contempt of court for violating a restraining order directing the union and its members to refrain from picketing and striking against the school corporation.

Then, by affirmation of the lower court's ruling, the Supreme Court concluded:

We thus see that both the federal and state jurisdictions and men both liberal and conservative in their political philosophies have uniformly recognized that to allow a strike by public employees is not merely a matter of choice of political philosophies, but is a thing which cannot and must not be permitted if the orderly function of our society is to be preserved (*Id.* at 18).

Other succinct excerpts extracted from the case report follow:

(1) The terms of employment are not subject to bargaining and strike pressure because they

237

are set by the legislative body and are not within the discretion of the agency which is the employer.

(2) To say that public employees can strike is to say that they can deny the authority of government.

(3) A strike by public employees is a strike against government itself, a situation so anomalous as to be unthinkable.

(4) Public employees occupy a status entirely different from private employees because they are agents of the government serving a public purpose and a strike by them contravenes the public welfare and results in paralysis of the society. (*Id.* at 19-20).

4. *Pinellas County Classroom Teacher Association v. Board of Public Instruction*, 214 So.2d 34 (Fla. 1968).

The legal principle that education is a governmental function and that teachers are governmental employees and subject to the laws pertaining thereto was exemplified in this case where a statewide teacher stoppage was interpreted by the Supreme Court of Florida as a *strike* by public school teachers and could be enjoined.

The teachers' association challenged the validity of the statute which "prohibits governmental officers and employees from participating in strikes against the government." The court pointed out that "the statute guarantees the right to bargain as a member of a union or labor organization but precludes the right to strike against the government" (*Id.* at 36).

The court rejected a contention that the injunctive relief granted the school board amounted to "involuntary servitude" and stated:

> We are not here confronted by an arbitrary mandate to compel performance of personal service against the will of the employee. These people were simply told that they had contracted with the government and that they could, if they wished, terminate the contract legally or illegally, and suffer the results thereof. They could not, however, strike against the government and retain the benefits of their contract positions.
>
> The teachers here were not quitting their jobs or severing the employer-employee relationship. They were free to do that before and after the injunction. What they were really attempting to do here was to exert pressure on the School Board by refusing to go to work, but at the same time laying claim to their positions and asserting the right to go back to work on terms more acceptable to them (*Id.* at 37).

5. *Rockwell v. Board of Education of Crestwood*, 226 N.W.2d 596 (Ct. of App. of Mich. 1975).

The teachers, members of the Crestwood Educational Association (CEA), refused to report for work. The situation thus remained in limbo until September 3, 1974, when plaintiffs initiated an action in Wayne County Circuit Court. They sued as homeowners and taxpayers in the district and as the parents of school children in the district. Their complaint requested that the board and teachers be ordered to bargain in good faith. It was also requested that the teachers be ordered to return to work and that the board be enjoined from firing the teachers (*Id.* at 597-98).

The case is complicated by the fact that the court found that the board "discharged the striking teachers in a procedurally improper manner." However, only the excerpt referring to legality of the strike is dealt with here:

It is well settled that there is neither a common law nor a constitutional right of public employees to strike. Moreover, in this State public employees are specifically denied the power to strike by Section 2 of the public employment relations act.

That act defines a public employee as, among others, a person "in the public school service." It is undisputed that these teachers are public employees subject to the provision of the act:

"Strike means the concerted failure to report for duty, the wilful absence from one's position, the stoppage of work, or the abstinence in whole or in part from the full, faithful, and proper performance of the duties of employment, for the purpose of inducing, influencing, or coercing a change in the conditions, or compensation, or the rights, privileges, or obligations of employment."

The circuit court panel found, and we agree, that the teachers were engaged in a strike prohibited by the act . . . (*Id.* at 598-99).

§ 8.2 Judicial view on sanctions.

1. *Board of Education v. New Jersey Education Association*, 53 N.J. 2d, 247 A.2d 867 (1968).

The judiciary considers "sanctions" to be comparable to the "strike" as a strategem to force school boards to accede to certain teacher demands. In the instant case, the court ruled that work stoppage actions by the teacher were illegal even though the less offensive word "sanctions" was used instead of "strike."

The landmark decision in this case was so pertinent and conclusive, that the excerpt from the court's opinion is quoted at considerable length as follows:

> Defendants deny there was a "strike." They seek to distinguish the usual concerted refusal to work from what transpired here. As to the teachers employed by the Board, defendants say they merely resigned as of a future date, and with respect to the interference with the Board's recruitment of replacements, defendants, as we understand them, say a refusal to accept employment is inherently different from a quit. But the subject is the public service, and the distinctions defendants advance are irrelevant to it, however sizeable they may be in the context of private employment. Unlike the private employer, a public agency may not retire. The public demand for services which makes illegal a strike against government inveighs against any other concerted action designed to deny government the necessary manpower, whether

241

by terminating existing employments in any mode or by obstructing access to the labor market. Government may not be brought to a halt. . . .

Hence, although the right of an individual to resign or to refuse public employment is undeniable, yet two or more may not agree to follow a common course to the end that an agency of government shall be unable to function. Here there was such collective action by agreement both as to the quitting and as to new employment. As to the mass resignations, an agreement to that end must be inferred from the very adoption by the members through their teachers union of the program of sanctions which, despite some verbal obscurity in this regard, quite plainly imparts an understanding to withdraw services when the union officialdom "imposes sanctions" upon a school district. The use of "unethical" in condemning new employment because of working conditions must mean it is also "unethical" to continue an existing employment under the same conditions. The full understanding must be that upon the imposition of sanctions, all services will be withdrawn. . . . Although the Board accepted the resignations and hence does not ask that that work stoppage be ended, we are satisfied the stoppage was concerted action to an illegal end.

And with respect to blacklisting of the school district and the scheme of "sanctions" upon teachers who offer to take employment with a "sanctioned" school board, it can escape no one that the purpose is to back up a refusal of others to continue to work. At a minimum the object is to withhold additional services a school district may need to discharge its public duty, which, as we have said, is no less illegal. Such an illegal agreement may come into being at the time of the strike or may antedate it. If individuals enter into a union or association on terms that upon the occurrence of some stipulated event or signal they will impede government in its recruitment of services, that very arrangement constitutes an agreement the law denounces. An agreement not to seek, accept, or solicit employment in government whenever the upper echelon of the union makes a prescribed pronouncement is, no less than an accomplished shutdown, a thrust at the vitality of government, and comes within the same policy which denounces a concerted strike or quit or slowdown or other obstruction of the performance of official duties (*Id.* at 872-73).

§ 8.3 Imposition of penalties.

Despite the generally accepted legal principle that teachers' strikes are illegal, teachers continue to strike, with the belief that they will not be prosecuted for doing so. There are instances, however, where teachers suffer a penalty for participating in strike movements.

1. *In re Brown,* 50 N.J. 435, 236 A.2d 142 (1967).

In this case the Supreme Court of New Jersey upheld the conviction and a $500 fine of a teacher for contempt of court when a temporary restraining order issued against a threatened strike against the Newark school system was ignored. The strike was called and the defendant teacher, along with some 1,700 others, did not report for work.

In support of its ruling the court made the following statement:

> Defendant contends the charge was not proved. He concedes that he was served with the restraining order, that he decided not to report to work, and stayed away. He says, however, that he did not report, although opposed to the strike, because if he had, his membership on the negotiating team would likely have been terminated, and with it his chance to seek an end to the stoppage. ... But the facts, indeed defendant's own testimony, show his violation of the order was willful. The real thrust of his appeal is that his motive was good. Good motive, of course, does not negate willfulness. Nor does it excuse an intentional breach of a court's order; it cannot rest with the individual to decide that he can accomplish a greater good by ignoring the restraint (236 A.2d at 143).

2. *National Education Association v. Lee County Board of Public Instruction,* 299 F. Supp. 834 (M.D. Fla., 1969).

In this case plaintiff teachers, joined by the National Education Association and the Florida Education Association, contested the legality of certain fines paid by approximately 400 public school teachers in Lee County, Florida.

As attempts were made to pass legislation necessary to meet demanded salary increases "thousands of teachers signed resignations, thus presaging a work stoppage."

The resigned teachers indicated their willingness to return to the classrooms providing they would be employed on the same basis as if their resignations had never been submitted or received. The Board, however, refused such conditions and insisted that "any such teachers shall forfeit a fine of $100." Two teachers who refused the fine were not permitted to return. They contended that the imposition of the fine as a condition to accepting their return to employment "violated the right to due process of law which is guaranteed to them by the Fourteenth Amendment to the United States Constitution" (*Id.* at 837).

In holding for the plaintiff teachers, the court commented as follows:

> There is no doubt in this Court's mind that punishment so imposed does not conform with requirements of due process of law. It would be difficult to imagine a more arbitrary action of government than the *ad hoc* imposition of a penalty for a wrong which had not been previously defined either by the imposing authority or by the legislature, for which there was no legislatively specified penalty and

which was imposed without any process or procedure. ... While the Board did not impose the fine directly, it was made a condition to the teachers' returning to work. However, this indirection cannot save the exaction. What the government may not do directly, it may not do indirectly by making it a condition on the granting of a privilege. ... Thus the fact that the fine in this case was made a condition of the teachers' return, rather than having been imposed directly on each teacher who resigned, gives its imposition no constitutional grace (*Id.* at 840).

3. *Joint School District No. 1, City of Wisconsin Rapids v. Wisconsin Rapids Education Association*, 234 N.W.2d 289 (Wis. 1975).

In this case an action was taken by teachers challenging the legality of the board's action in fining them $10 a day for violating a temporary injunction restraining a strike. Of the 350 teachers in the district, 213 were advised of the order, but they refused to go back to their classrooms. Consequently "the board closed all schools in the district because of an inadequate number of teachers to conduct classes in any meaningful manner."

In its complaint, the board alleged that a strike had been initiated by defendants, that the strike was illegal, and that, as a result, it could not operate the school system. The board further alleged that the citizens and taxpayers in the district were suffering irreparable harm as a result of the illegal strike and that there existed no adequate remedy at law. In its prayer for judgment, the board requested that an order be issued permanently restraining and enjoining the defendants from continuing the strike and related activities (*Id.* at 293).

After hearing much testimony pro and con, the court ruled in favor of the school district, and stated in conclusion:

> It appears clear that the statute envisions a penalty which may continue until the order for injunction is obeyed. In imposing the penalty, the trial court provided that the striking teachers would be liable for the $10 fine for each day.... They did not return on January 16 and the fines were imposed.
>
> All of the orders appealed from should be affirmed except the order finding 317 teachers in contempt. The contempt finding and fines pursuant thereto should be limited to the 213 teachers notified of the injunction, and fines collected from those in excess of the 213 should be remitted. Further, upon remand, if the record as now made reveals any of the 213 teachers notified of the injunction did in fact comply with it, their contempt findings should be reversed and fines remitted (*Id.* at 307).

4. *Hortonville Joint School District v. Hortonville Education Association,* 96 S. Ct. 2308 (1976).

According to a landmark decision of the United States Supreme Court, in 1976, school boards have the

constitutional right to fire illegally striking teachers
with whom they are negotiating a work contract.

By a 6 to 3 vote, the justices reversed a decision of the
Wisconsin Supreme Court that the Hortonville, Wis.
school board exceeded its power by discharging striking
teachers.

The Hortonville Education Association and six fired
teachers contended that the board's action was a denial
of due process of law because the board was too
involved in the dispute to give them a fair trial.

In reversing the decision of the Supreme Court of
Wisconsin, Chief Justice Burger who delivered the
opinion of the High Court, emphasized that:

> The Board's decision whether to dismiss
> striking teachers involves broad con-
> siderations, and does not in the main turn
> on the Board's view of the "seriousness" of the
> teachers' conduct or the factors they urge
> mitigated their violation of state law. It was
> not an adjudicative decision, for the Board had
> an obligation to make a decision based on its
> own answer to an important question of policy:
> what choice among the alternating responses
> to the teachers' strike will best serve the
> interests of the school system, the interests of
> the parents and children who depend upon the
> system, and the interests of the citizens whose
> taxes support it? The Board's decision was
> only incidentally a disciplinary decision; it had
> significant governmental and public policy
> dimensions as well.

State law vests the governmental or policy making function exclusively in the School Board and the State has two interests in keeping it there. First, the Board is the body with overall responsibility for the governance of the school district; it must cope with the myriad day-to-day problems of a modern public school system including the severe consequences of a teachers' strike; by virtue of electing them the constituents have declared the Board members qualified to deal with those problems, and they are accountable to the voters for the manner in which they perform. Second, the state legislature has given to the Board the power to employ and dismiss teachers, as a part of the balance it has struck in the area of municipal labor relations; altering those statutory powers as a matter of federal due process clearly changes that balance. . . . (*Id.* at 2316).

Respondents have failed to demonstrate that the decision to terminate their employment was infected by the sort of bias that we have held to disqualify other decisionmakers as a matter of federal due process. A showing that the Board was "involved" in the events preceding this decision, in light of the important interest in leaving with the Board the power given by the state legislature, is not enough to overcome the presumption of honesty and integrity in policymakers with decisionmaking power (*Id.* at 2316).

Mr. Justice Stewart, with whom Justices Brennan and Marshall joined, dissented and made the following concluding statement:

> Under a realistic appraisal of psychological tendencies and human weaknesses, I believe that there is a constitutionally unacceptable danger of bias where school board members are required to assess the reasonableness of their own actions during heated contract negotiations that have culminated in a teachers' strike. If, therefore, the respondents' interpretation of the state law is correct, then I would agree with the Wisconsin Supreme Court that "the board was not an impartial decisionmaker in a constitutional sense and that the [teachers] were denied due process of law" (*Id.* at 2317).

§ 8.4 Right to picket.

1. *Board of Education of Community Unit School District v. Redding*, 207 N.E.2d (Sup. Ct. of Ill., 1965)

The right to picket is frequently associated with the right to strike. In the instant case a teachers' union contended that picketing is a form of speech and when conducted in a peaceful and truthful manner it is immune from restraint, regulation and control.

In rejecting this contention the Supreme Court of Illinois stated:

> However, the premise that peaceful picketing is immune from all regulation and control is a false one. While picketing has an

ingredient of communication, the cases make it clear that it cannot be dogmatically equated with constitutionally protected freedom of speech, and that picketing is more than free speech because picket lines are designed to exert, and do exert, influences which produce actions and consequences different from other modes of communication. . . . Indeed, these by-products of picketing which go beyond free speech are self-evident in this case. It is now well established that the latter aspects of picketing may be subject to restrictive regulations, and while the specific situation must control decision, it is more than clear that a State may, without abridging the right of free speech, restrain picketing where such curtailment is necessary to protect the public interest and property rights and where the picketing is for a purpose unlawful under State laws or policies, whether such policies have been expressed by the judicial organ or the legislature of the State (*Id.* at 431).

The picketing here, though peaceful, was for the purpose of fostering and supporting an unlawful strike against a governmental employer and, being for an unlawful purpose, should have been enjoined for this reason alone. Apart from this, however, the effect of the influences exerted by the picketing was to impede and obstruct a vital and important governmental function — the proper and efficient education of our children — making its curtailment necessary to protect the patently overriding public interest (*Id.* at 432).

Chapter 9
LIABILITY FOR PUPIL INJURY

§ 9.1 Non-immunity for teachers.

The cloak of immunity for tort liability, applicable to school districts and school board members, does not cover teachers. The reason for this is that school board members, as *public officials*, enjoy a sovereign status; whereas teachers are merely *public employees* and therefore liable for their tortious acts as are all other citizens not holding public office.

1. *Miller v. Jones*, 224 N.C. 783, 32 S.E.2d 594 (1945).

The above-stated legal principle was evidenced in this early non-school case, where the Supreme Court of North Carolina reasoned that:

> The mere fact that a person charged with negligence is an employee of others to whom immunity from liability is extended on grounds of public policy does not thereby excuse him from liability for negligence in the manner in which his duties are performed, or for performing a lawful act in an unlawful manner. The authorities generally hold the employee individually liable for negligence in the performance of his duties, notwithstanding

the immunity of his employer, although such negligence may not be imputed to the employer on the principle of respondent superior, when such employer is clothed with governmental immunity under the rule (32 S.E.2d at 597).

§ 9.2 Negligence as a factor.

The great majority of liability cases against the teacher have to do with *negligence*, which is considered to be any conduct which falls below standard for the protection of others against unreasonable risk of harm. Inadequate supervision, such as absence from the classroom, has frequently been considered by the courts as negligence of the teacher. However, it has been held as unreasonable for the teacher to be present in the classroom *at all times under all circumstances*.

1. *Cirillo v. Milwaukee*, 34 Wis. 2d 705, 150 N.W.2d 460 (1967).

This is a case in point where a physical education teacher, after checking the attendance instructed the boys to shoot baskets while he was to be absent for a short time. During the teacher's absence the playing became rough and developed into "rowdyism" which resulted in serious injury to one of the students. Consequently, action was taken by the student against the teacher for the injuries sustained during the teacher's absence. A lower court ruled that the teacher was negligent and liable, but the Supreme Court of Wisconsin reversed the decision, indicating its rationale in doing so, as follows:

It does not seem inherently unreasonable to expect that teachers will be present in classes which they are entrusted to teach. This should not, of course, mean that a teacher who absents himself from a room is negligent as a matter of law. As this court said, the teacher's duty is to use "reasonable care." What this means must depend upon the circumstances under which the teacher absented himself from the room. Perhaps relevant consideration would be the activity in which the students are engaged, the instrumentalities with which they are working (band saws, dangerous chemicals), the age and composition of the class, the teacher's past experience with the class and its propensities, and the reason for and duration of the teacher's absence (150 N.W.2d at 465).

Finally, it is contended on behalf of the defendants that to permit a recovery by plaintiffs under these circumstances would be to constitute the defendants the insurer of the safety of Milwaukee school children. The trial court was of this opinion. While it is true this court has recognized that a teacher is neither immune from liability nor is he an insurer of his students' safety, he is liable for injuries resulting from his failure to use reasonable care (*Id.* at 466).

2. *Dailey v. Los Angeles Unified School District,* 84 Cal. Rptr. 325 (1970).

According to this case, supervision of a student by a teacher at school could not be expected to be greater than it would be by a parent at home.

Facts of the case indicate that two boys who were friends were engaged in "slap boxing" during the lunch period. (Slap boxing is a form of boxing in which *open hands* are used instead of *clenched fists*.) One of the boys fell backwards when slapped, suffering a fractured skull which resulted in his death a few hours later.

Parents of the boy brought action against the school district and two teachers who were responsible for supervising the school grounds. In holding for the teachers, the court mentioned that "principal's duty to supervise Edward Downey was no greater than was that of Downey's parents," and had the incident occurred at the boy's home the parents, like the teachers, would have been helpless in avoiding the accident.

The court reasoned that:

> There was no evidence of a "specific propensity" of Edward Downey to intentionally harm anyone else or to engage in conduct creating an unreasonable risk of harm to anyone else. We cannot see how a parent of Edward Downey, had the parent been unaware that Edward Downey ever slap boxed with anyone, could have been liable for Michael's death if the slap boxing had occurred without the actual knowledge of the parent in the background of the parent's home. Without knowledge of any "specific propensity" of

Edward Downey to slap box (and this assumes that slap boxing could be found to create an unreasonable risk of harm to the participants) and without knowledge that the slap boxing was occurring, it cannot be said that the parent should know of the necessity . . . for exercising such control (*Id.* at 329).

The court then added that:

. . . if the principal knew or should have known of the necessity of exercising control over Edward Downey because of his propensity to slap box, a jury could well have found the principal liable. But there was no evidence that Edward had a specific propensity to slap box. Thus neither the principal nor any teacher had any duty "to control the conduct of" Edward during the lunch hour on the facts before us (*Id.* at 330).

§ 9.3 Assault and battery as a factor.

Disciplinary practices which are more severe than moderate administration of corporal punishment in accordance with statutory provisions, sometimes may be referred to as *assault and battery*. The line of distinction may be narrow.

1. *Frank v. Orleans Parish School Board,* 195 S.2d 451 (La. 1967).

In this case it was held that a physical education teacher's *excessive* disciplinary action subjected him to liability and a requirement to pay damages in the amount exceeding $11,000. In support of its decision, the court stated:

Henderson's [the teacher's] action in lifting, shaking and dropping the boy were clearly in excess of that physical force necessary to either discipline or to protect himself, and subjects the defendants to liability for the injuries incurred as a result thereof (*Id.* at 453).

The difficulties encountered in differentiating between corporal punishment for purposes of maintaining discipline and committing assault and battery are expressed in the following statement by the Court of Appeals of Louisiana, Fourth Circuit:

We expressly refrain from making any judicial pronouncement as to whether it is actionable *per se* for a teacher in a public school to place his or her hands upon a student. Common sense would dictate, however, that the individual facts and environmental characteristics emanating from each case would disclose both the right and the reason for a teacher to do so, and the degree of force, if any, which may be used under particular or peculiar circumstances. A general rule in the negative relative to this problem may encourage students to flaunt the authority of their teachers. On the other hand, a general rule permitting physical contact between teacher and student in any instance without qualification would obviously encourage the one who occupies a position of superiority to take advantage of those who are in a less favorable position since they are subject to their authority (*Id.* at 453-54).

2. *Gonyaw v. Gray*, 361 F. Supp. 366 (U.S.D.C. D. Vermont 1973).

The main aspects of this case were discussed in Chapter 4, Section 3, dealing with the administration of corporal punishment. Here the constitutionality of a Vermont statute was challenged which provides:

A teacher or principal of a school or a superintendent or a school director on request of and in the presence of the teacher, may resort to any reasonable form of punishment, including corporal punishment, and to any reasonable degree, for the purpose of securing obedience on the part of any child enrolled in such school, or for his correction, is for the purpose of securing or maintaining order in and control of such school (*Id.* at 368).

The plaintiffs argued that: "the statute violates the Fourteenth Amendment due process requirement in its substantive aspect." The Court disagreed and stated that: " 'liberty,' as guaranteed by the Fourteenth Amendment, does not guarantee the freedom of a school child from the reasonable imposition of school discipline" (*Id.* at 369).

The court went on to say:

The extent to which a teacher may engage in corporal punishment is limited in Vermont by the availability of civil and criminal penalties for its abuse. The statute gives a teacher the right when necessary to maintain discipline moderately to chastise his pupils; but if the punishment is excessive or improper, the teacher is guilty of assault and battery.... Beyond this deterrent, a teacher who exceeds statutory limits in administering corporal punishment is answerable to the parents of the child, not only in the courts, but also he may be called upon to respond through the school board, the parents' elected representatives (*Id.* at 370).

As indicated above, community participation in school affairs and the possibility of legal action serve to deter the arbitrary imposition of corporal punishment upon students. The mere fact that a statute vests an official with discretion in seeking legitimate objectives does not render the statute void for vagueness merely because the possibility exists that discretion may be abused. There may be borderline cases in which it is difficult to determine where the facts will fall, but such indefiniteness will not condemn the statute (*Id.* at 370).

3. *Roberts v. Way,* 398 F. Supp. 856 (U.S.D.C.D. Vermont 1975).

As revealed in this case, there is a distinction between *assault* and *discipline.* Here the court stated:

It is established in Vermont that "a school-teacher has the right, when necessary to maintain discipline, moderately to chastise his pupils; but, if the punishment is excessive or improper, the teacher is guilty of assault and battery" (*Id.* at 860).

The language of the statute permits resort only to reasonable forms of punishment, within the bounds of moderation, and free from any element of cruelty. The statute is merely declaratory of the prevailing law of tort liability on the subject of corporal punishment in the schools of the country.

> In *Gonyaw* this court held that where an administered punishment bears a closer relation to assault than to a considered act of discipline, an adequate remedy exists within the Vermont courts.... According to the factual allegations of this complaint, the punishment inflicted on the plaintiff bears a closer relation to assault than to a considered act of discipline. The plaintiffs' complaint states a cause of action under Vermont law for assault and battery. The plaintiffs' allegations that defendant Way's kicks caused "severe bruises" to Michael's abdomen, back and legs is analagous to the *Melen* fact situation. In *Melen*, a Vermont jury found a public school teacher guilty of assault and battery for striking an eleven-year-old girl in the area of the kidney with the edge of an arithmetic book, causing a muscle spasm in her back. Under *Melen* and *Gonyaw* both Michael and his mother have an adequate remedy at state law for money damages (*Id.* at 861).

4. *Jerry v. Board of Education*, 376 N.Y.S.2d 737 (App. Div. 1975).

In this case a teacher's dismissal was upheld on grounds that the teacher used excessive force (assault and battery) on some students.

One parent had "complained that Mr. Jerry had pulled her second-grade daughter's hair . . . and that Jerry had used profanity while discussing the incident with her by phone (*Id.* at 740).

> . . . other incidents were reported by children who said that they had been eyewitnesses to petitioner's conduct. Among the acts described were the striking of children with dodge balls, soccer balls, hands and fists, the throwing or pushing of children against walls and floors so as to cause them to strike their heads and knees, the pulling of hair, the lifting up and carrying of children by the neck, and the pulling of a child by the ear. Some children cried and shook with fear and sought permission to stay in their homeroom (*Id.* at 744).

In commenting on its ruling the court made the following statement:

> That the penalty of dismissal has a grave impact on petitioner is obvious. But, by his actions he manifested a disregard for the School Board's right and duty to make and enforce policies fostering the physical, emotional and educational well-being of students, the good-will and confidence of their parents, and the orderly administration of schools. Nor was petitioner's misconduct

limited to a single isolated instance ... rather
it was a persistent course of conduct in
defiance of clear and repeated warnings. In
these circumstances, we cannot say that the
penalty was disproportionate to the offenses
... (*Id.* at 745).

§ 9.4 Unsuccessful claims for immunity.

In many tort cases where teachers have been alleged
to be liable for their negligent and imprudent acts,
causing pupil injury, the courts have absolved the
teachers. On the other hand, where a teacher's
negligence or unreasonable behavior has been found to
be the proximate cause of a pupil injury, the courts have
found the teacher liable. Therefore, when the facts of a
case prove that a pupil's injury is because of a teacher's
negligence or imprudent action, the teacher may seek
some legal loophole whereby he might be held immune
from liability and free from paying money damages.
The three most common pleas for the teacher's
immunity are (1) the *in loco parentis* status, (2) the
master-servant relationship, and (3) employment in a
governmental function.

1. *Morris v. Ortiz*, 103 Ariz. 119, 437 P.2d 652 (1968).

In the eyes of the court, the *in loco parentis* status is
a weak defense because even a parent can be held liable
for child mistreatment which causes injury. For example, in the instant case, the Supreme Court of
Arizona stated:

The relationship of a public school teacher to
his pupil is in some respects in loco parentis.

Having the right to control and supervise the pupil, there is a correlative duty to act as a reasonable and prudent parent would in like circumstances. The rationale of in loco parentis does not however apply in determining liability for a negligent tort against the pupil. In most jurisdictions the parent is not liable for negligent tort against his child, but the public school teacher may be.

The problem lies in determining what criteria should be used to meet the standard of care necessary to be exercised by the public school teacher. If the probability of harm can be foreseen, the public school teacher should take such measures as are reasonable and prudent to prevent an injury to the student. . . . Teachers presumptively endowed with superior skill, judgment, intelligence and foresight, must fulfill the strong duties arising from their public position by exercising care commensurate with the immaturity of their charges and the importance of their trust (437 P. [2d] at 657-58).

2. *Kersey v. Harbin,* 531 S.W.2d 76 (Mo. Ct. of App. 1975).

The *in loco parentis* status, as a valid claim for teacher immunity from liability for pupil injury was also refuted by the Missouri Court of Appeals, as indicated by the following succinct statement:

Defendant's assertion that they stood in loco parentis to the decedent and therefore immune from suit has only superficial ingenuity to commend it. The notion that a teacher stands in place of a parent is a legal fiction intended to describe and limit the teacher's privilege to discipline the child. If the loco parentis doctrine still stands in the wake of *Baker v. Owen, supra*, it has never been thought to excuse the teacher for his negligence (*Id.* at 82).

3. *Smith v. Consolidated School District No. 2,* 408 S.W.2d 50 (Mo. 1966).

The claim that the master-servant relationship (*respondeat superior*) holds the school administrator, rather than the teacher, liable for a teacher's negligence resulting in pupil injury has *no* judicial support. For example, in the instant case, the Supreme Court of Missouri stated:

> The theory that Cradock, the physical education instructor, was an employee of Herndon, the Superintendent, and that Herndon would be liable for his acts in a master-servant relationship is wholly fallacious. It is a matter of public knowledge, and we may say of judicial nature, that all teachers in the public schools are employees of the school district and are employed by its contracts. The superintendent may presumably recommend, but he does not employ. He is neither the master nor the employer of any teacher (*Id.* at 53-4).

4. *Miller v. Jones, supra.*

The same legal principle was expressed by the Supreme Court of North Carolina when it reasoned that:

> The mere fact that a person charged with negligence is an employee of others to whom immunity from liability is extended on grounds of public policy does not thereby excuse him from liability for negligence in the manner in which his duties are performed, or for performing a lawful act in an unlawful manner. The authorities generally hold the employee individually liable for negligence in the performance of his duties, notwithstanding the immunity of his employer, although such negligence may not be imputed to the employer on the principle of respondeat superior, when such employer is clothed with governmental immunity under the rule (*Id.* at 597).

5. *Crabbe   v.   County   School   Board   of Northumberland County*, 164 S.E.2d 639 (Va. 1968).

A more common, but equally ineffective, defense is to claim that, since the school board is immune from liability by virtue of its sovereign status in the performance of a governmental function, the teacher should likewise be protected with immunity because teaching is a governmental function.

The reaction of the Supreme Court of Virginia to such a claim is expressed in the following manner:

> . . . in the operation of a school a school board is performing a governmental function and hence is immune from liability for personal

injuries by a pupil and caused by the alleged negligence of an instructor, employed at the school ... (*Id.* at 640).

Next, as to the liability of defendant Albrite (teacher and employee of the board): We do not agree with the contention of this defendant that the immunity of the School Board from liability to the plaintiff extends to him. It is true that at the time the plaintiff was injured through the alleged negligence of the defendant Albrite, the latter was employed in and performing his duties as an instructor in the school. But the fact that Albrite was performing a governmental function for his employer, the School Board, does not mean that he was exempt from liability for his own negligence in the performance of such duties (*Id.* at 641).

6. *Salyers v. Burkhart,* 339 N.E.2d 652 (Ohio 1975).

In this case action was brought against a shop teacher (Burkhart) and the board of education as a result of serious injury sustained by a student who was not adequately warned of the dangerous conditions that existed where he was welding.

A trial court found the board to be immune from tort liability while engaged in the performance of a governmental function. It held further that Burkhart did not act maliciously or deliberately, and was not liable in tort when acting within the scope of his employment involving the exercise of judgment and discretion.

The Court of Appeals affirmed the dismissal of the complaint filed against the board. However, it reversed the dismissal of the complaint against Burkhart, stating:

> We conclude that there is no Ohio authority which authoritatively extends the cloak of governmental immunity to a teacher, and that the general rule provides that teachers are individually liable for their own torts (*Id.* at 653).

Chapter 10

SEXUALITY AND THE TEACHER

§ 10.1 Legal limitations of sexual behavior.
§ 10.2 Academic freedom in treating sex matters.
§ 10.3 Marital regulations over teachers.

§ 10.1 Legal limitations of sexual behavior.

Innumerable cases concerning sexuality and the teacher have been adjudicated in recent years. The majority of them deal with questionable sexual behavior. (Several such cases have already been referred to in Chapter 6 in the section discussing "immorality" as a cause for teacher dismissal.)

Normally a teacher's illicit behavior outside the classroom is not just cause for dismissal if the teacher's reputation is not tarnished to the degree which would result in public resentment and disapproval. If, however, a teacher's sexual conduct, in or out of the school, is such that it establishes detrimental teacher-student relations the court would be inclined to uphold a school board's action in dismissing the offending teacher. The following case is illustrative.

1. *Erb v. Iowa State Board of Public Instruction,* 216 N.W.2d 339 (Iowa 1974).

In this case a complaint was made by a farmer (Johnson) against Erb (a teacher of physical education and senior class sponsor). The farmer charged that his wife who taught home economics in the same school and Erb were engaging in adulterous affairs, which was suspicioned by the frequent late-night absences from home by the "farmer's wife." Johnson's suspicions were substantiated by the observations he made, as described in the case report:

He suspected Margaret and Erb were meeting secretly and engaging in illicit activity in the Johnson automobile. One night in May he hid in the trunk of the car. Margaret drove the car to school, worked there for some time, and later drove to a secluded area in the country where she met Erb. Margaret and Erb had sexual intercourse in the back seat of the car while Johnson remained hidden in the trunk . . . (*Id.* at 341).

On the basis of the admitted evidence Johnson told the board his objective was *removal* of Erb from the school and not *revocation* of his teaching certificate. Nevertheless the board voted five to four to revoke Erb's certificate and the "trial court held Erb's admitted adulterous conduct was sufficient basis for revocation of his certificate . . ." (*Id.* at 342).

The Supreme Court of Iowa, however, ruled that "the board acted illegally in revoking the certificate, and supported its ruling on other court decisions which held that conduct must adversely affect the teacher-student relationship before revocation will be approved. There was no evidence of such adverse effect in the instant case.

In a concluding statement the Supreme Court supported Erb with the following words:

The evidence showed Erb to be a teacher of exceptional merit. He is dedicated, hard-working and effective. There was no evidence to show his affair with Margaret Johnson had or is likely to have an adverse effect upon his relationship with the school administration, fellow teachers, the student body or the community. . . . The conduct itself was not an open or public affront to community mores; it became public only because it was discovered with considerable effort and made public by others. (*Id.* at 344).

2. *Fisher v. Snyder,* 346 F. Supp. 396 (Neb. 1972).

The same judicial reasoning is expressed in this case where a divorcee who taught in a high school was known to have young men stay in her single bedroom apartment over nights.

An Avon lady testified that she visited and apparently got the teacher out of bed early one Saturday morning. Later a young man emerged from the bedroom. On the basis of that testimony, the board acted to dismiss the teacher for conduct "unbecoming a teacher."

A United States District Court held that the flimsy evidence produced did not justify sufficient cause for terminating the teacher's contract. The court's reasoning is evidenced in the following statements which are quoted in numerous succeeding cases dealing with similar issues.

> When viewed most favorably from the position of the board of education and taking every permissible inference from the testimony elicited in the hearing, there is simply no proof of impropriety in Mrs. Fisher's conduct which affected her classroom performance, her relationship with students under her care, or otherwise had any bearing

271

on any interest possessed by the board of education. At most, the evidence may be said to raise a question of Mrs. Fisher's good judgment in her personal affairs, when measured against an undefined standard which someone could suppose exists in a small town in Nebraska. I am constrained to hold that that was not enough to justify termination of the contract (*Id.* at 898).

Her effectiveness as a teacher, disciplinarian, or counselor stands without factual challenge. It is the lack of any factual, as contrasted with imagined or theoretical connection between Mrs. Fisher's association and a substantial weakening of the educational enterprise conducted by the board of education that must result in a finding that the termination of the contract was not constitutionally justified (*Id.* at 401).

3. *In re Grossman,* 127 N.J. Super. 13, 316 A.2d 39 (1974).

In this bizarre case, a male teacher of vocal music in an elementary school experienced a gender identity problem which worsened to the extent that he finally sought medical advice. He was diagnosed as a "transsexual"; that is, one who anatomically is born with the genitalia of one sex but who believes himself (or herself) to be a member of the other sex.

Although Grossman had notified his superiors of his impending absence for surgery, he did not disclose its nature until his return in late April or May of 1971, when he informed the township superintendent of schools and made known his intention of remaining in the school system as a female. After completing the academic year in male attire, he assumed the name of Paula Miriam Grossman and began to live openly as a woman.

During the summer of that year the matter was under active and continuous consideration by the board, looking toward a satisfactory resolution of the problem. A series of meetings took place between it and Mrs. Grossman (it seems appropriate to use the female gender henceforth), arrangements were made for her to be examined by board selected psychiatrists, and finally a proposal was submitted by the board to engage her on a one-year contract at the same pay to teach the same courses, but only on an elective basis in the high school, provided she would resign, thus relinquishing her tenure, and obtain a new certificate in her female name. The offer was rejected (316 A.2d at 42).

After hearing much testimony and many opinions from professional personnel and reviewing the conflicting evidence on the issue, the Commissioner of Education finally reached "his conclusion that Mrs. Grossman's presence in the classroom could potentially result in psychological harm to students" (*Id.* at 45).

In support of the Commissioner's ruling for the dismissal of Mrs. Grossman, the Superior Court of New Jersey reasoned as follows:

> We think it would be wrong to measure a teacher's fitness solely on his or her ability to perform the teaching function and to ignore the fact that the teacher's presence in the classroom might, nevertheless, pose a danger

of harm to the students for a reason not related to academic proficiency. We are convinced that where, as has been found in this case, a teacher's presence in the classroom would create a potential for psychological harm to the students, the teacher is unable properly to fulfill his or her role and his or her incapacity has been established within the purview of the statute. In fairness to Mrs. Grossman, we emphasize that the Commissioner's conclusions relate only to her fitness to continue teaching in the Bernards Township school system. We express no opinion with respect to her fitness to teach elsewhere and under circumstances different from those revealed in the present case (*Id.* at 49).

4. *Wishart v. McDonald,* 367 F. Supp. 530 (Mass. 1973).

This case involved a 43-year-old male who was employed as a sixth grade teacher for five years before he was dismissed for public "conduct unbecoming a teacher by displaying and fondling in public view a dress mannequin."

Among the charges for conduct unbecoming a teacher were the following:

(a) That you have on various occasions displayed and carried a dress mannequin in the public view on your Spooner Street property, having dressed said mannequin in feminine attire, and have on occasion caressed said mannequin.

(b) That your actions in the public view on your Spooner Street property in regard to the dressing and undressing of said dress mannequin in feminine attire have been on various occasions of a suggestive or lewd nature (*Id.* at 532).

Although not denying the charges, the plaintiff teacher argued that the evidence indicates "his conduct in no way relates to his ability to function as a teacher and that to dismiss him for this unrelated conduct was impermissible." In fact, witnesses rated him as an above-average or even "excellent" teacher.

The court concluded that, on the basis of evidence presented, the school committee had not "acted arbitrarily or capriciously in its action." Moreover, the plaintiff's contention that he was deprived of his constitutional right of privacy was denied, as indicated in the following statement of the court:

The court is not impressed by plaintiff's argument that the defendant's actions constituted an unconstitutional invasion of his right to privacy. However convincing his argument may be that private sexual conduct is protected from governmental intrusion, the evidence in this case is ample that on various occasions the conduct was public in nature or at least was carried on with such reckless disregard of whether or not he was observed that it lost whatever private character it might have had (*Id.* at 535).

275

§ 10.2 Academic freedom in treating sex matters.

During the past decade teachers — especially those who teach literature — have been carried into the courts because of their reference to the "four lettered word" meaning sexual intercourse. When teachers assign readings which include the taboo word, parents and board members may take action by dismissal with potential litigation to follow.

1. *Keefe v. Geanakos,* 418 F.2d 359 (1st Cir. 1969).

The first applicable case on the issue was adjudicated in a federal court, after a teacher gave to each member of his senior English class a copy of a controversial article, "The Young and the Old," written by a psychiatrist and professor at a noted medical school. A highly offensive word in the article was an alleged vulgar term for an *incestuous son.* As a result, the teacher was suspended by the board of education.

In defense of the teacher, the United States Court of Appeals made the following statement, which served as a legal precedent for other later cases dealing with the same issue:

> The Lifton article, which we have read in its entirety, has been described as a valuable discussion of "dissent, protest, radicalism and revolt." It is in no sense pornographic. We need no supporting affidavits to find it scholarly, thoughtful, and thought-provoking. The single offending word, although repeated a number of times, is not artificially introduced, but, on the contrary, is important to the development of the thesis and the conclusions of the author.

... It is not possible to read the article, either in whole or in part, as an incitement to libidinous conduct, or even thoughts. If it raised the concept of incest, it was not to suggest it, but to condemn it; the word was used, by the persons described, as a superlative approbrium. We believe not only that the article negatived any other concept, but that an understanding of it would reject, rather than suggest, the word's use.

With regard to the word itself, we cannot think that it is unknown to many students in the last year of high school, and we might well take judicial notice of its use by young radicals and protesters from coast to coast.

Hence the question in this case is whether a teacher may, for demonstrated educational purposes, quote a "dirty" word currently used in order to give special offense, or whether the shock is too great for high school seniors to stand. If the answer were that the students must be protected from such exposure, we would fear for their future. We do not question the good faith of the defendants in believing that some parents have been offended. With the greatest respect to such parents, their sensibilities are not the full measure of what is proper education (*Id.* at 361-62).

2. *Parducci v. Rutland,* 316 F. Supp. 352 (Ala. 1970). Just one year after *Keefe,* the issue of sexual obscenity was again litigated. The controversy involved in this case arose because of an assignment, as outside

reading in an English class, of a story entitled
"Welcome to the Monkey House" which was comic
satire written by a prominent author. It was chosen by
the teacher to explain "one particular genre of western
literature."

School officials, who admitted they possessed no
expertise in the field of literature, were very critical of
the assignment and described it as "literary garbage."
As a consequence the board dismissed the teacher from
his job for assigning materials which had a "disruptive
effect on the school."

The plaintiff teacher asserted in his complaint that his
dismissal for assigning the controversial reading was in
violation of his First Amendment right. The court
agreed with the teacher's complaint and emphasized
that "the right to teach, to inquire, to evaluate and to
study is fundamental to a democratic society" (*Id.* at
355).

In its ruling the court added:

> Since the defendants have failed to show
> either that the assignment was inappropriate
> reading for high school juniors, or that it
> created a significant disruption to the
> educational processes of this school, this Court
> concludes that plaintiff's dismissal constituted
> an unwarranted invasion of her First
> Amendment right to academic freedom. (*Id.* at
> 356).

By way of expressing its concern as to the absence of
standards involved in the instant case, the court
continued:

When a teacher is forced to speculate as to what conduct is permissible and what conduct is proscribed, he is apt to be overly cautious and reserved in the classroom. Such a reluctance on the part of the teacher to investigate and experiment with new and different ideas is anathema to the entire concept of academic freedom (*Id.* at 357).

3. *Mailloux v. Kiley,* 323 F. Supp. 1387 (Mass. 1971).
The issue of using the "four-lettered word" was litigated again in a federal court. And again a United States District Court upheld a teacher's action against a school board which discharged him for writing a slang word for sexual intercourse on the blackboard, and in discussing such word as a taboo word before this eleventh grade class. The teacher wrote on the board the controversial four-lettered word, and asked for volunteers to define it. After a couple minutes of silence, a boy volunteered that the word meant "sexual intercourse." There followed a brief discussion of taboos in English after which the teacher, without using the word orally, went on to other matters.

After relying on the legal precedents set forth in the two preceding cases discussed here, the court expressed the opinion that:

> . . . a teacher who uses a taboo sexual word must take care not to transcend his legitimate professional purpose. When a male teacher asks a class of adolescent boys and girls to define a taboo sexual word the question must not go beyond asking for verbal knowledge and become a titillating probe of privacy. He

279

must not sacrifice his dignity to join his pupils as "frere et cochon." Here it should be stated unequivocally, there is no evidence that this plaintiff transcended legitimate professional purposes. Indeed the court has specifically found he acted in good faith (*Id.* at 1391).

In support of a qualified right of a teacher, even at the secondary level, to use a teaching method which is relevant and in the opinion of experts of significant standing has a serious educational purpose in the central rationale of academic freedom. The Constitution recognizes that freedom in order to foster open minds, creative imaginations, and adventurous spirits. Our national belief is that the heterodox as well as the orthodox are a source of individual and of social growth. We do not confine academic freedom to conventional teachers or to those who can get a majority vote from their colleagues. Our faith is that the teacher's freedom to choose among options for which there is any substantial support will increase his intellectual vitality and his moral strength. The teacher whose responsibility has been nourished by independence, enterprise, and free choice becomes for his student a better model of the democratic citizen. His examples of applying and adapting the values of the old order to the demands and opportunities of a constantly changing world are among the most important lessons he gives to youth (*Id.* at 1391).

4. *State v. Board of School Directors of Milwaukee,*
14 Wis.2d 243, 111 N.W.2d 198 (1961).

The three cases referred to in this section indicate
that the courts uphold the teacher in the treatment of
sex matters where the purpose has a relevant, worthy
and wholesome purpose. However, a teacher is not
likely to have judicial support by discussing sexual
matters before students in a manner that is irrelevant,
oppressive and degrading. The instant case is
illustrative.

Here a tenure teacher was dismissed from his job for
discussing sex with a senior class in speech at a boys'
technical school in a manner which was considered by
the school board to be improper. The offending teacher
(a) explained procedures at houses of prostitution, (b)
explained techniques of performing sex acts as if
recounting personal experience, (c) condoned pre-
marital sexual relations, (d) related vulgar stories, and
(e) treated other aspects of sex in an improper,
irrelevant and unwholesome manner.

The court upheld the school board's dismissal of the
teacher and in so doing offered the following rationale:

> ... if relator's discourses on sex in his speech
> classes had been conducted in such a manner
> as to constitute proper conduct in a biology
> class, they would not automatically have been
> converted into misconduct warranting
> discharge by the happenstance that they took
> place in a speech class, absent any rule of the
> school authorities prohibiting the same or any
> specific warning to relator from the principal
> or superintendent that sex was not to be a

subject of discussion in speech classes. However, if relator's manner of discoursing on the topics of sex in his speech classes exceeded the bounds of the recognized standards of propriety, we deem that it constituted bad conduct which would warrant a discharge even though there was no express rule prohibiting it and he had received no warning to desist therefrom. As an intelligent person trained to teach at the high school level, relator should have realized that conduct was improper (111 N.W.2d at 206-7).

5. *Simon v. Jefferson Davis Parish School Board,* 289 So.2d 511 (La. App. 1974).

In a later case a high school teacher sought action for judicial review of his dismissal for certain charges of statements made before his class, such as:

A. Integration in churches and classrooms came recently, but in bed for a long time because if a white man wanted a little loving he would go across the tracks.

B. The black man has had the idea that only white women could love adequately because of picture shows.

C. Black girls have more illegitimate children because they can't afford to have anything done as white girls do.

D. Obscenity and vulgarity are needed to motivate people (*Id.* at 515).

The Court of Appeals of Louisiana affirmed the lower court's ruling which upheld the board for dismissal of the offending teacher. The court said, in part:

... the appropriateness of certain actions is oftentimes dictated by the nature of the position held by an individual. More specifically a classroom teacher, merely by the nature of that position, should be aware of the impropriety of some practices. ... We believe that the findings noted above are examples of acts which need no regulation to define their decorum.

Plaintiff contends that the statements made by him to his class are protected by his constitutional right of free speech, and by the right of academic freedom enjoyed by public school teachers.

To this contention, the court responded as follows:

We conclude that the first and second noted statements made by the plaintiff clearly served no serious educational purpose, and are therefore not entitled to protection. Moreover, without more connexity and relevancy than has been shown it is impossible for us to state that the school board and lower court erred ... (*Id.* at 517).

In recent years school officials and personnel have been challenged for the selection and use of textbooks containing alleged obscenities. The issue has caused much disturbance and animosity in some communities as was illustrated by the shameful proceedings which occurred in West Virginia in 1974. Surprisingly there has not been much actual litigation on the issue that has been reported by courts of record. The following case, however, indicates how the judiciary views the trends in textbook selection and censorship.

6. *Grosser v. Woollett,* 45 Ohio Misc. 15, 341 N.E.2d 356 (Ct. of Com. Pl. 1974).

Here the plaintiffs asked the court to issue a permanent injunction restraining and enjoining the defendants (school officials and personnel) from using or assigning the books "Manchild in the Promised Land" by Claude Brown and "One Flew Over the Cuckoos Nest" by Ken Kesey. The "Cuckoo" book was particularly singled out as containing obscenities unfit for children to read.

In commenting on the complaints of the plaintiffs, the court emphasized that:

> It is certain that many words and phrases used compelled the plaintiffs to bring this action. It is also certain that the plaintiffs are probably not aware of the full contents of the records of the decisions of the Supreme Court of the United States that have, to a large extent, made it possible for the current literature, magazines, etc., to include much matter that had previously been outlawed.

> The use of words and descriptions of occurrences that a very few years ago were objectionable and shocking, at times even unlawful, now are commonplace and some are definitely not even taboo . . . (*Id.* at 359-60).

In projecting the trend further, the court went on to state:

> Within the past few years the attitude of the people generally has changed with reference to books, literature, the use of words and the

description of incidents therein that were previously taboo. Such changes may well continue in the same pattern in the future. It may possibly be that ultimately legislative bodies or the Supreme Court of the United States will determine that all persons, juveniles and adults, may legally be exposed to what are now illegal books and writings and the description or narration of heretofore taboo actions such as is not now the status of Ohio laws the decisions of the courts or current attitudes of the members of the local communities (341 N.E.2d at 366).

§ 10.3 Marital regulations over teachers.

Unlike circumstances of today, some years ago school boards wrote provisions in the teacher's contract declaring a teacher subject to dismissal if marrying while in service. And in some instances such provisions were judicially condoned.

1. *Richards v. District School Board,* 78 Ore. 621, 153 P. 482 (1915).

Judicial approval of the "no marriage" policy came to an end in 1915 when the Supreme Court of Oregon upheld a teacher who married despite the school board regulation which stipulated:

Married women shall not be eligible to positions as teachers in the district except by special resolution of the board. All women teachers who marry during their time of service, thereby terminate their contracts with the district (153 P. at 482).

The school board's dismissal of the teacher for violating the rule was declared illegal for the reasons stated below:

> Efficiency and competency of teachers and the welfare of the schools are of course consummations "devoutly to be wished." If a teacher becomes inefficient or fails to perform a duty, or does some act which of itself impairs usefulness, then a good or reasonable cause for dismissal would exist. The act of marriage, however, does not, of itself furnish a reasonable cause. . . . The reason advanced for the rule adopted by the board is that after marriage a woman may devote her time and attention to her home rather than to her home work. It is impossible to know in advance whether the efficiency of any person will become impaired because of marriage, and a rule which assumes that all persons do become less competent because of marriage is unreasonable because such a regulation is purely arbitrary. If a teacher is just as competent and efficient after marriage, a dismissal because of marriage would be capricious. If a teacher is neglectful, incompetent, and inefficient, she ought to be discharged whether she is married or whether she is single (153 P. at 485-86).

2. *Drake v. Covington County Board of Education,* 371 F. Supp. 974 (Ala. 1974).

The eligibility of *unwed* pregnant teachers has become a litigious issue in recent years. This is the first case recorded on the issue where an unwed pregnant teacher was successful in a dismissal suit, where the board dismissed her on an "immorality" charge.

Ignoring the charge of "immorality" the court upheld the teacher on her right of privacy in sexual matters such as deciding "to bear or beget a child." The courts rationale for its decision follows:

> The Board made no finding that Drake's claimed immorality had affected her competency or fitness as a teacher, and no such nexus was developed in the evidence. No "compelling interest" as to the cancellation vel non of Drake's contract of employment was established by the evidence which would justify the invasion of Drake's constitutional right of privacy. Under the testimony that Drake was in the early months of pregnancy, she in consultation with her physician would be free to determine, without regulation by the State, whether pregnancy should be terminated. For the State, in the absence of any compelling interest, to base cancellation of Drake's employment contract on evidence growing out of her consultations with her physician was, in our opinion, an unconstitutional invasion of her right of privacy (*Id.* at 979).

One judge made a lengthy and vigorous dissent to the majority ruling from which the brief excerpt follows:

> In the instant case, there was evidence from which the Board may have found that Miss

Drake was immoral and that such conduct interfered with her teaching ability. The Board found her guilty of "immorality," in the word used by the statute without specifying whether it implicitly found a nexus with her teaching ability. Her claim that her sexual conduct was private paled when she admitted that it was publicly discussed in Florala. Rumor of immorality of a public school-teacher in a small town travels fast and has a larger impact on the educational process than in a city. It is difficult to see how a Court can require of a Board composed of laymen the niceties of charging and making special findings of everything that may be required in the way of constitutional niceties, particularly when those requisites are not called to their attention. Rather, it seems more appropriate to me that the Plaintiff, having the burden of proof should be required to prove that her discharge was constitutionally defective. The technical defect, right of privacy, on which the majority relies, was not pointed out so that the Board might call for and specifically consider evidence thereof at the time of the hearing. It is difficult for this Court to learn from the evidence how Miss Drake's secret first became a public rumor associated with a public figure. It is enough to interfere with operation of a school system that it did (*Id.* at 981-82).

3. *Andrews v. Drew Municipal Separate School District,* 371 F. Supp. 27 (Miss. 1973).

This case developed from a contested local school board policy which forbade employment of school personnel who are *unwed* parents. The plaintiffs in the case contended that the board policy or practice was violation of equal protection because it creates an unconstitutional classification to sex.

In ruling against the school officials by granting injunctive relief to the plaintiffs, the court commented as follows:

> ... Certainly, no school administrator or board should be precluded from denying employment to any one determined to be of bad moral character upon a fair and unbiased consideration of pertinent information, and we do not make the slightest intimation otherwise. After a careful review of Drew's policy and relevant evidence, however, we hold that the policy or practice of barring an otherwise qualified person from being employed, or considered for employment, in the public schools merely because of one's previously having had an illegitimate child has no rational relation to the objectives ostensibly sought to be achieved by the school officials and is fraught with insidious discrimination; thus it is constitutionally defective under the traditional, and most lenient, standard of equal protection and violation of due process as well. Alternatively, the policy, both inherently and as applied, constitutes an impermissible, discriminatory classification based upon sex (*Id.* at 31).

The court went on to point out the unreasonableness of the policy because:

> . . . it conclusively presumes the parent's immorality or bad moral character from the single fact of a child born out of wedlock. By the rule, a parent, whether male or female, who has had such a child, would be forever precluded from employment. Thus, no consideration would be given to the subsequent marriage of the parent or to the length of time elapsed since the illegitimate birth, or to a person's reputation for good character in the community. A person could live an impeccable life, yet be barred as unfit for employment for an event, whether the result of indiscretion or not, occurring at any time in the past. But human experience refutes the dogmatic attitude inherent in such a policy against unwed parents (*Id.* at 33).

4. *Kornblum v. Newark Unified School District,* 37 Cal. App. 3d 623, 112 Cal. Rptr. 457 (1974).

In recent years the marital regulations over teachers have been mainly focused on *mandatory maternity or sick leave rules. Kornblum* is a typical case involving a probationary teacher who defied a school district rule that the pregnant teacher must go on maternity leave "three months prior to the expected birth of the child and is to be continued to the end of the school year during which the leave is granted. *In no event* may the employee return to work less than three months following the birth of the child" (112 Cal. Rptr. at 458).

It was found by the court that:

> Plaintiff had experienced no medical problems related to her pregnancy and had been advised by her doctor that she could continue working as a teacher up until the child was born and could resume teaching two weeks after giving birth. She did in fact resume teaching on a substitute basis, in another school district, two weeks after her child was born.
>
> Plaintiff had desired to continue teaching right up until the birth of her child and to resume teaching as soon thereafter as her doctor thought permissible. . . . (*Id.* at 458).

The defendant school district, however, notified the plaintiff teacher, in writing, that she *would not* be recommended for re-employment. The court ruled that the school district's action was illegal and stated:

> In the instant case, it is apparent that the requirement of rule "K" that a teacher go on maternity leave three months prior to the expected birth date of her child is unconstitutional and therefore invalid. The same is likewise true of the provision precluding a teacher who has gone on maternity leave from resuming her employment within three months of the birth of her child (*Id.* at 459).

5. *Cleveland Board of Education v. La Fleur,* 94 S. Ct. 791 (Ohio 1974) and 6. *Cohen v. Chesterfield County School Board,* 94 S. Ct. 791 (Va. 1974).

After going through the entire judicial hierarchy, the issue of *mandatory* leave for pregnant teachers reached a climax when the United States Supreme Court granted *certiorari* for two companion cases, and ruled in favor of two pregnant teachers who refused to abide by the board policy which required a pregnant teacher to take *unpaid* maternity leave five months before expected childbirth and to continue until the next regular semester after the child is three months old. The teachers, in each instance, insisted on teaching until approximately a month before "expectancy" and to resume teaching as soon as they felt able to do so.

An introductory excerpt from the court's opinion is stated as follows:

> This court has long recognized that freedom of personal choice in matters of marriage and family life is one of the liberties protected by the Due Process Clause of the Fourteenth Amendment.

> By acting to penalize the pregnant teacher for deciding to bear a child, overly restrictive maternity leave regulations can constitute a heavy burden on the exercise of these protected freedoms. Because public school maternity leave rules directly affect "one of the basic civil rights of man," . . . the Due Process Clause . . . requires that such rules must not needlessly, arbitrarily, or capriciously impinge upon this vital area of a teacher's constitutional liberty (*Id.* at 796).

One argument stated by the board to adopt the mandatory rule was: to keep the pregnant teacher out of the classroom during the specified final months of pregnancy to protect the health of the teacher and her unborn child. With respect to this reason stipulated by the board, the court responded as follows:

> . . . question is whether the rules sweep too broadly. That question must be answered in the affirmative, for the provisions amount to a conclusive presumption that every pregnant teacher who reaches the fifth or sixth month of pregnancy is physically incapable of continuing. There is no individualized determination by the teacher's doctor — or the school board's — as to any particular teacher's ability to continue at her job. The rules contain an irrebuttable presumption of physical incompetency, and that presumption applies even when the medical evidence as to an individual woman's physical status might be wholly to the contrary (*Id.* at 798).

The second reason set forth by the board was that the rules provided for "continuity." The court's rejection of that argument follows:

> Were continuity the only goal, cut-off dates much later during the pregnancy would serve as well or better than the challenged rules, provided that ample advance notice requirements were retained. Indeed, continuity would seem just as well attained if the teacher herself were allowed to choose the date upon which to commence her leave, at least so long as the decision were required to be made and notice given of it well in advance of the date selected (*Id.* at 797).

In sum, the majority opinion of the United States Supreme Court is stated as follows:

> We conclude, therefore, that neither the necessity for continuity of instruction nor the state interest in keeping physically unfit teachers out of the classroom can justify the sweeping mandatory leave regulations that the Cleveland and Chesterfield County School Boards have adopted. While the regulations no doubt represent a good-faith attempt to achieve a laudable goal, they cannot pass muster under the Due Process Clause of the Fourteenth Amendment, because they employ unrebuttable presumptions that unduly penalize a female teacher for deciding to bear a child (*Id.* at 800).

Justice Rehnquist, joined by Chief Justice Burger, offered a brief dissent which ended with the following sentence:

> If legislative bodies are to be permitted to draw a general line anywhere short of the delivery room, I can find no judicial standard of measurement which says the ones drawn here were invalid (*Id.* at 806).

7. *Danielson v. Board of Higher Education,* 358 F. Supp. 22 (N.Y. 1972).

Some unusual court cases can evolve from the 1972 Civil Rights Act, especially where "leaves" are concerned. For example, in this case, a lecturer in sociology at the University of New York, applied for a paternal leave to care for his newborn son. Since his wife, who also was a lecturer planned to go back to work immediately following the birth, Danielson wanted to stay home for *six* months (with pay afforded a mother as provided for maternity leave) to care for the infant.

In denying Danielson's application for leave, the court made the following statement:

> The essence of Danielson's claim is that women faculty members are permitted to take a leave of absence in connection with pregnancy, up to three semesters, for the purpose, among others, of caring for a newborn infant, without adversely affecting their tenure rights, but the same child care leave privilege is denied to men (*Id.* at 24).

> Mr. Danielson's primary claim is that his right to equal protection of the laws has been violated by defendant's refusal to extend to him the same child care leave privilege which they extend to women solely because he is a man. He claims that by so discriminating against men who seek to fully participate in the care of their children, defendants are effectively denying men the right to play a full and equal role in their families. He then argues that the fact that child care has traditionally been considered women's work is no more an answer here than were the use of such sex stereotypes in an attempt to bar women from certain kinds of employment (*Id.* at 27).

The University filed a motion to strike Danielson's complaint, but, significantly, Judge Baker for the United States District Court, S. W. New York, denied the motion, holding that "the complaint stated a good cause for action."

Of course Mr. Danielson would have had a much stronger case had he actually borne the child himself.

Chapter 11

CONCLUSIONS

Part I: The Student

§ 11.1 Compulsory and prohibitory school attendance.
§ 11.2 Authority over curricular activities.
§ 11.3 Regulatory control over the student.
§ 11.4 Student disciplinary practices.

§ 11.1 Compulsory and prohibitory school attendance.

Early court decisions indicated that the public concept was that parents should be granted complete discretionary control of the education of their children — including school attendance. After much litigation over the issue, however, the courts decided that the state has sufficient power to enact compulsory school attendance legislation.

Alternatives to public school attendance have never been absolute. For example, in the precedential *Pierce* case, the United States Supreme Court ruled that attendance at a *qualified private* school instead of a *public* school is legal. Also home instruction has judicial sanction, providing the home instruction is equivalent to that which would be attainable in a public school.

Vaccination as a condition for attendance is an issue that has been frequently litigated. Courts generally hold that parents are guilty of violating the compulsory school attendance laws even when the children are sent to school but denied admission because of failure to meet the vaccination requirements.

The majority of cases evolving from violation of vaccination requirements are based upon religious beliefs. However, the courts hold to the legal principle

297

that "liberty of conscience is one thing; license to endanger the lives of others by practice contrary to statutes passed for public safety and reliance upon modern medical knowledge is another."

Attendance status of unwed pregnant students has been a litigated issue during the past decade. In 1969, two young unwed mothers challenged à school board's policy of excluding them from school attendance as a violation of the due process and equal protection clauses of the Fourteenth Amendment. In upholding the girl's complaints the court held they could not be excluded from school attendance unless "they were found to be so lacking in moral character that their presence in the school would taint the education of other students." The court expressed the opinion that exclusion from school attendance would deprive them of the opportunity for rehabilitation and for seeking higher education.

Attendance and assignment discrimination because of race became a closed legal issue when the United States Supreme Court rendered a unanimous decision in the famous *Brown* case of 1954. The High Court upheld the contention that segregation in and of itself causes inferiority and is thus a denial of due process and equal protection guaranteed by the United States Constitution.

The ruling in *Brown* raised the question as to how desegregation of the races in the public schools could be legally accomplished. The judiciary decided that *busing of pupils* would be most effective in many areas. The decision in the very controversial *Swann* case upholds the busing of pupils and requires school districts to do so *unless* some other more effective tool is conceived and applied.

Attendance and assignment discrimination because of sex as a legal issue has not reached the courts of record in many instances. In the most recent case on the issue a female high school student gained admission to an academically superior boys' school despite the board's objection. The court enjoined the board from refusing to admit the girl or any other member of the class she represents "solely on the basis of sex."

§ 11.2 Authority over curricular activities.

Prescriptions of certain subjects are usually made by local and state school boards of education, and less frequently by state legislatures. The earliest cases dealt mainly with the allocation of authority between school officials and parents in determining what the pupils should study. At first the courts applied the common law principle that parents held supreme authority during the minority of their children. More recently the courts have upheld state authorities in determining curricular content unless in conflict with state or federal law.

Restrictive attempts against instruction of certain subjects have been focused mainly on the teaching of evolution and sex education. After much litigation in the lower courts, the issue of *teaching evolution* was presumably put to rest when the United States Supreme Court ruled, in *Epperson,* that legislation prohibiting it, because of its supposed conflict with Biblical accounts, was contrary to the mandate of the First and Fourteenth Amendments to the Constitution. Of the several cases adjudicated in courts of last resort, the issue of having *sex education* in the curriculum, the courts have been in agreement that sex education is legal within legislative limitations. The compulsory aspects of the program have been resolved by an "excusal" provision which permits those whose parents object, to absent themselves from the instruction.

Regulations concerning loyalty display have frequently been the cause for litigation. The requirements for students to salute the flag have been most vigorously contested. In the first case on the issue the United States Supreme Court ruled (in *Gobitis*) that the requirement was legal as a means of achieving a feeling of national unity. In a subsequent case (*Barnette*) the United States Supreme Court reversed the decision in *Gobitis,* holding that the requirement transcends constitutional limitations and invades the sphere of intellect and spirit which it is the purpose of the First Amendment to preserve from all official control.

The federal courts have likewise ruled that a student has the constitutional right to exhibit disrespect for our flag and country by refusing to stand and participate in the pledge of allegiance.

Regulations concerning religious instruction apply mainly to Bible reading and recitation of prayers. *Reading of the Bible* has been litigated continuously for more than a century. With the vaccilation of state courts on the issue, the United States Supreme Court finally ruled in the famous *Schempp* case (1963) that statutes requiring that reading of verses from the Bible at morning exercises are unconstitutional.

Recitation of prayers in the public schools has likewise been ruled by the Supreme Court to be unconstitutional. The High Court, in *Engel-Vitale* (1962) ruled that a brief state-mandated prayer was inconsistent with the Establishment Clause of the First Amendment, and therefore unconstitutional.

Despite continuous opposition to the judicial repudiation of reciting prayers in the public schools, it is not probable that the Supreme Court is likely to reverse its stand. It is noteworthy that only one Judge dissented in the Bible reading case and the prayer case. Some statesmen, and others, advocate amendment of the United States Constitution to legalize the practice. That is not likely to happen in the foreseeable future.

Released time for religious instruction became a practice because of the judicial restrictions to pursue religious instruction in the public schools. In the first case (*McCollum*) which went to the United States Supreme Court, the program as conducted in the Champaign schools was declared illegal because of the mingling of religious education in the public schools during public school time.

In a following United States Supreme Court case (*Zorach v. Clauson*) it was held that a released-time program as conducted in the New York City program was valid. As contrasted with the Champaign plan, there was (1) neither supervision nor approval of religious teachers; (2) no solicitation of pupils or distribution of cards; (3) the religious instruction was conducted outside the school building and grounds.

Several cases concerning the released-time issue have been adjudicated since *McCollum* and *Zorach*, but in virtually all instances the judicial decisions have followed the precedent set down in *Zorach*.

§ 11.3 Regulatory control over the students.

Student grooming has been one of the more litigious issues governing the student in recent years. In the early court cases school officials were upheld in their regulations regarding hair styles. Gradually, however, the regulations were regarded by the judiciary as being invalid, unless the hair styles were so extreme as to cause disruption in the classroom. In recent years courts have expressed reluctance to deal with the issue but feel required to do so when the deprivation of constitutional rights is challenged.

Display of insignia as a protest gesture was most common when students were prompted to protest their participation in the Vietnam war. The landmark case (*Tinker*) established the legal principle that display of symbolic insignia such as wearing black armbands is constitutionally permissible. The United States Supreme Court ruled that the display of insignia is akin to pure speech — a constitutional right guaranteed by the First Amendment.

Other instances of symbolic display as evidenced in the "button cases" were also judicially approved when the wearing of buttons was done in a manner without causing disruption of classes or school routine.

Student demonstrations are likewise viewed by the courts as a form of expression, protected by the First Amendment, "unless shown likely to produce a clear and present danger of serious substantive evil that arises far above public inconvenience, annoyance, or unrest."

Freedom of speech and press is less likely to be an issue for litigation in the secondary schools than in institutions of higher learning. Most of the applicable cases have to do with the issuance and dissemination of written materials which are allegedly detrimental to the school. Here again the higher courts condone the students' right to express their views in written form unless done in a manner and degree which "would substantially disrupt or materially interfere with school procedures."

Search and seizure presents a legal issue which frequently occurs when school personnel search students or student lockers for the purpose of suppressing the possession of marijuana and other harmful drugs. The courts condone such action as a means of protecting the student body.

The search of student lockers is held lawful even though the student may have control of his locker against fellow students; that control does not prevent school officials from inspecting the lockers for evidence of containing harmful substances.

Restraining affiliation with secret societies has triggered numerous court cases. In virtually all instances the courts have held anti-fraternity rules to be legal on the grounds that school administrators consider secret societies have a deleterious influence and are inimical to the best interests of the school.

Barring married students from non-classroom activities was upheld as proper authority of a school board in the earlier cases. More recently, however, the courts have voided school regulations which prevent married students from participation in *all* school activities. The judicial view is that marriage should be encouraged rather than living together unmarried, and that a student may not be penalized for entering the marriage status which is sanctioned by state law.

Sex discrimination in sports has been outlawed due to the provisions of Title IX of the Education Amendments of 1972. The federal ban provides that students or others may not be excluded from participation in any phase of the educational program receiving federal financial assistance.

Consequently, in cases which have been adjudicated thus far, the courts have held that rules which prohibit girls from participating with boys in sports events cannot stand, by virtue of the fact that such prohibition is in violation of the Fourteenth Amendment.

§ 11.4 Student disciplinary practices.

Application of the in loco parentis doctrine usually enters into the legal issue of disciplining the student. At first the doctrine was applied in cases where teachers attempted restraint and correction of unruly students. However, the doctrine has lost much of its original intention where school authorities have extended its application to other areas of control involving the student.

Due process rights of students acquired impetus with the United States Supreme Court decision in *Gault* (discussed in Chapter 4 of this publication). In essence that decision means that before a juvenile can be found guilty and penalized he must be accorded the same due process rights accorded adults, such as: (1) notices of the charges; (2) right to counsel; (3) right to confrontation and cross-examination of the witnesses; (4) privilege against self-incrimination; and (5) right of appellate review.

Administration of corporal punishment was formerly the most common method of disciplining unruly students. Although it is still practiced in some school systems it has been declining as a disciplinary tool. In fact it has been statutorily banned in two states and prohibited by state boards of education in several other states.

304

When it is allowable and practiced the courts generally hold that it must (1) be in conformance with statutory enactment; (2) be for the purpose of correction without malice; (3) not be cruel or excessive; and (4) be suited to the age and sex of the pupil.

Suspension and expulsion have been used more and more as a means of disciplining students since strict limitations have been placed upon the administration of corporal punishment. The legal principle is now firmly established that school authorities may suspend or expel from school any student who disobeys a reasonable rules or regulation within statutory limits. However, there are very definite legal limits (such as time) in the exclusionary practices.

The main question concerned the length of time a student could be expelled from school without first being afforded all the formal procedures of due process. That issue reached a climax in *Goss* v. *Lopez* when the United States Supreme Court held that students suspended for even *short periods* of time were nevertheless entitled to minimal due process under the Fourteenth Amendment.

Deprivation of awards and privileges as a disciplinary device is generally voided by the courts. For example, students who were denied their diplomas for refusing to wear ill-fitting garments at the graduation exercise were upheld by the court and the board was required to issue the diploma.

Humiliation as a punitive measure is frowned upon by the judiciary. Although teachers frequently resort to such tactics, it is seldom that it results in actual litigation. In the one case referred to in this publication, the court held the view that humiliation of a student

305

before his classmates can be more deleterious than the
infliction of physical pain and cannot have legal
sanction.

Part II: The Teacher

§ 11.5 Right of association.

The right of association, as a legal issue, had very
little impact before communism threatened our public
schools. Then anti-subversive laws were enacted and
litigated. The most stringent and litigated of these laws
were the Feinberg Law of New York State and the Ober
Law of Maryland. They were intended to ferret out
those teachers in the school systems who were affiliated
with the Communist Party. At first the lower courts
declared them unconstitutional, but later their
constitutionality was upheld by higher courts. Most
recently, however, the United States Supreme Court
ruled that the Feinberg Law is in violation of the
Federal Constitution.

Invoking the Fifth Amendment has sometimes been
tried by teachers who have been suspected of affliation
with subversive organizations when questioned by
legislative investigating committees. Several court
decisions, one of which was rendered by the United
States Supreme Court, indicate that a teacher is subject
to dismissal when refusing to answer such questions
when asked to do so by a legally-constituted committee.

Testifying against one's associates has been litigated only once in a court of last resort. There the court ruled that although teachers may be required to answer questions concerning their own affiliation with subversive organizations, they may not be required to disclose the names of presently-employed teachers known to be or having been members.

§ 11.6 Grounds for teacher dismissal.

Immorality is frequently cited and litigated as a cause for teacher dismissal. Although the intended scope of the word's meaning may not be defined, the courts usually consider alleged moral conduct only to the extent that it is, in some way, inimical to the welfare of the school community. In comparing court decisions of today with those of several decades ago, it is apparent that social attitudes regarding morality have changed markedly. Acts which were previously regarded as immoral may be no longer so regarded.

Incompetency appears to be the most frequent cause for teacher dismissal. That is partially because the term encompasses such a broad scope of actions or inactions that almost any wrongdoing might be considered as incompetency. Even though the incompetency of a teacher may be beyond the teacher's control, school boards and courts consider it a just cause for dismissal if serious enough to impair the school programs. Welfare of the pupil takes precedence over that of the teacher.

Insubordination has been interpreted by the courts as the willful refusal of a teacher to obey reasonable rules and regulations of school officials. The refusal by a teacher to accept a non-classroom assignment has often been alleged as insubordination. But it may not be so regarded by the judiciary if the extra assignment bears no relation to the school's program, or if it is foreign to the nature of duties for which the teacher was originally employed.

Grooming violations have to do mostly with tonsorial appearance. Hair styles, whiskers and goatees, prohibited by school board regulations have frequently been cause for teacher dismissal to be followed by litigation. Unless a teacher's grooming is so remote from the mode as to disrupt student morale and behavior, a school board regulation pertaining thereto would not have judicial sanction.

Although the courts generally uphold teachers who violate school regulations prohibiting the wearing of whiskers, goatees, or flamboyant hair styles, they are most likely to uphold a dress code prohibiting the wearing of unconventional clothing.

§ 11.7 Teachers' rights outside the classroom.

Engaging in political campaigns is not very common for school teachers. The few cases that have been adjudicated over the issue indicate that the teacher has that right as well as does any other citizen. However, the courts will not extend that right to be exercised in a classroom with a captive audience.

Holding public office such as "dual office holding" by school personnel has frequently been the subject of litigation. While it is a well recognized legal principle that one may not serve as a *local school board member* while holding a "public office" at the same time, that principle, however, does not apply to a teacher. The reason, of course, is that a school board member is a *public officer* whereas a teacher is regarded by the courts to be a *public employee.*

Expressing opinions on public issues is a constitutional right afforded teachers, as well as other citizens. However, the time, place and manner in which critical opinions are expressed raise questions of legality. In the one landmark case (*Pickering*), the United States Supreme Court upheld the right of teachers to publicly criticize certain actions of the school board. The High Court reasoned that since teachers are "as a class" the members of a community most likely to have informal and definite opinions as to how funds should be allotted, to the operation of the school, "it is essential that they be able to speak out freely on such questions without fear of retaliatory dismissal."

Refusing non-classroom assignments is closely associated with the extracurricular activities. The judicial view on the issue is that the education of children is no longer confined to the four walls of a classroom for a restricted number of hours. Consequently, teachers may be expected to discharge certain duties beyond the classroom and regular class hours. On the basis of court cases reviewed on this subject it is noted that, legally, the extra assignment must be *reasonable*: it (1) must not require excessive hours beyond the normal teaching period; (2) must have some relation to the teacher's interests, abilities and certification; (3) must be made with a purpose beneficial to pupils; (4) must not be discriminatory; and (5) must be professional in nature.

309

§ 11.8 Right to strike.

Judicial reaction to teachers' strikes was first expressed in 1951 in the *Norwalk* case. Even though often ignored, the court opinion in that early case is still applicable today. Generally courts hold that although teachers have the right to resign they do not have the legal right to strike, unless permitted to do so by statute. The following reasons are: (1) education is a public function; (2) teachers are governmental employees; and (3) governmental employees do not have a legal right to strike.

Judicial view on sanctions is similar to that as on strikes. The judiciary considers sanctions to be comparable to the strike as a stratagem to force school boards to accede to certain teacher demands. The landmark New Jersey case, referred to in Chapter 8, indicates that work stoppage by a group of teachers is illegal regardless of whether being prompted by a strike or sanctions.

Imposition of penalties for striking teachers is rare because of its likelihood to deplete the teacher supply. Nevertheless fines have in some instances been imposed upon individual teachers and teachers' unions.

The landmark decision by the United States Supreme Court in *Hortonville,* in 1976, indicates that school boards have the constitutional right to fire illegally striking teachers with whom they are negotiating a work contract.

Right to picket is associated with the right to strike. The judiciary rejects the argument that the right to picket is akin to "free speech," but declares that it is illegal because its intent is to impede and obstruct the important governmental function to educate our children.

§ 11.9 Liability for pupil injury.

Non-immunity for teachers in pupil injury cases has no legal support when the pupil's injury is due to the negligence of the teacher. The cloak of immunity for tort liability, applicable to school board members, does not cover teachers — the reason being that school board members have sovereign status as *public officials,* whereas teachers are merely *public employees.*

In addition to *negligence* as being cause for liability injury cases, a teacher may be held liable for pupil injury resulting from unwarranted *assault and battery.* Charges in such cases usually stem from administration of corporal punishment.

Unsuccessful claims for immunity of teachers are usually as follows: (1) the relationship of a teacher to the pupil is analogous to that of a parent to his child (*in loco parentis*); (2) because of a master-servant relationship (*respondeat superior*), the school administration, rather than the teacher, should assume the liability; and (3) since the school board is immune against liability by virtue of its sovereign status in the performance of a governmental function, the teacher shall likewise be protected by immunity because teaching is a governmental function. Generally, the courts hold that *none of the above claims are valid.*

§ 11.10 Sexuality and the teacher.

Legal limitations of sex behavior of teachers have been frequently litigated in recent years. Of the cases reviewed on the issue, the courts have indicated that the illicit sexual behavior outside the classroom is not just cause for dismissal if the teacher's reputation is not tarnished to the degree that would result in public resentment and disapproval. If, however, a teacher's sexual conduct, in or out of the school, establishes detrimental teacher-student relations the judiciary would be inclined to uphold the board's dismissal of the offending teacher.

Academic freedom of treating sex matters is a live legal issue. Teachers of literature especially have been carried to the courts for assignments and discussions of readings which include the four-lettered taboo word and other alleged obscene expressions.

Courts generally uphold the teacher who discusses sexual matters if they have a relevant meaning. However, a teacher is not likely to have judicial support for discussing sexual matters before students in a manner that is irrelevant, oppressive and degrading.

TABLE OF CASES

Board of Education of City of New York v. Allen, 6 Misc.2d 453, 167 N.Y.S.2d 221 (1956), § 5.5.

Board of Education of Community Unit School District v. Redding, 207 N.E.2d 427 (Sup. Ct. of Ill. 1965), § 8.4.

Board of Education of El Monte School District v. Calderon, 35 Cal. App. 3d 492, 110 Cal. Rptr. 916 (1974), § 6.2.

Board of Education for Logan County v. Akers, 243 Ky. 177, 47 S.W.2d 1046 (1932), § 7.1.

Braxton v. Board of Public Instruction of Duval County, Florida, 303 F. Supp. 958 (M.D. 1969), § 6.5.

Brenden v. Independent School District, 742, 342 F. Supp. 1224 (Minn. 1972), § 3.9.

Brown, In re, 50 N.J. 435, 236 A.2d 142 (1967), § 8.3.

Brown v. Board of Education, 347 U.S. 483, 74 S. Ct. 686 (1954), § 1.6.

Burnside v. Byars (Miss.), 363 F.2d 744 (1966), § 3.2.

Burton v. Cascade School District Union High School No. 5, 353 F. Supp. 254 (Ore. 1973), § 6.2.

Butts v. Dallas Independent School District, 436 F.2d 728 (1971), § 3.2.

Celestine v. Lafayette Parish School Board, 284 So.2d 650 (La. 1973), § 4.6.

Chilton v. Cook County School District No. 207, Maine Township, 26 Ill. App. 3d 459, 325 N.E.2d 666 (1975), § 4.1.

Cintron v. State Board of Education, 384 F. Supp. 674 (D. P. R. 1974), § 3.4.

Cirillo v. Milwaukee, 34 Wis.2d 705, 150 N.W.2d 460 (1967), § 9.2.

Citizens for Parental Rights v. San Mateo County Board of Education, 51 Cal. App. 3d 1, 124 Cal. Rptr. 68 (Court of Appeals First District, Division 2, 1975), § 2.2.

Cleveland Board of Education v. La Fleur, 94 S. Ct. 791 (Ohio 1974), § 10.3.

Cohen v. Chesterfield County School Board, 94 S. Ct. 791 (Va. 1974), § 10.3.

Conyers v. Pinellas County Board of Public Instruction (Fla. Cir. Ct. No. 16, 634, 1969), § 4.2.

Epperson v. Arkansas, 393 U.S. 97, 89 S. Ct. 266 (1968), § 2.2.

Erb v. Iowa State Board of Public Instruction, 216 N.W.2d 339 (Iowa 1974), § 10.1.

Farrell v. Joel, 437 F.2d 160 (2d Cir. 1971), § 4.2.

Fernald v. City of Ellsworth Superintending School Committee, 342 A.2d 704 (Sup. Jud. Ct. of Me. 1975), § 6.4.

Ferrell v. Dallas Independent School District (Tex.), 261 F. Supp. 545 (1966), § 3.1.

Finot v. Pasadena City Board of Education, 58 Cal. Rptr. 520 (1967), § 6.5.

Fisher v. Snyder, 346 F. Supp. 396 (Neb. 1972), § 10.1.

Fortman v. Texarkana School District No. 7, 514 S.W.2d 720 (Sup. Ct. of Ark. 1974), § 4.4.

Frain v. Baron, 307 F. Supp. 27 (U.S.D.C. E.D.N.Y. 1969), § 2.3.

Frank v. Orleans Parish School Board, 195 S.2d 451 (La. 1967), § 9.3.

Gault, In re, 387 U.S. 1 (1967), § 4.2.

Gere v. Stanley (Pa.), 320 F. Supp. 852 (1970), § 3.1.

Gilbertson v. McAlister, 403 F. Supp. 1 (D.C. Conn. 1975), § 6.4.

Gilpin v. Kansas State High School Activities Association, Inc., 377 F. Supp. 1233 (Kan. 1974), § 3.9.

Goetz v. Ansell, 477 F.2d 636 (C.A.N.Y. 1973), § 2.3.

Goldsmith v. Board of Education of Sacramento, 66 Cal. 157, 225 Pac. 783 (1924), § 7.1.

Gonyaw v. Gray, 361 F. Supp. 366 (U.S.D.C. D. Vermont 1973), § 9.3.

Goss v. Lopez, 95 S. Ct. 729 (Ohio 1975), § 4.4.

Graber v. Kniola, 52 Mich. App. 269, 216 N.W.2d 925 (1974), § 3.1.

Griffin v. Tatum (Ala.), 300 F. Supp. 60 (1969), § 3.1.

Grosser v. Woollett, 45 Ohio Misc. 15, 341 N.E.2d 356 (Ct. of Com. Pl. 1974), § 10.2.

Grossman, In re, 127 N.J. Super. 13, 316 A.2d 39 (1974), § 10.1.

Guerrieri v. Tyson, 147 Pa. Super. 239, 24 A.2d 468 (1942), § 4.1.

Guthrie v. Board of Education of Jefferson County, 298 S.W.2d 691 (Ky. 1957), § 6.3.

Joint School District No. 1, City of Wisconsin Rapids v. Wisconsin Rapids Education Association, 234 N.W.2d 289 (Wis. 1975), § 8.3.

Kaplan v. School District of Philadelphia, 388 Pa. 213, 130 A.2d 672 (1957), § 5.4.

Keefe v. Geanakos, 418 F.2d 359 (1st Cir. 1969), § 10.2.

Kelley v. Ferguson, 95 Nev. 63, 144 N.W. 1039 (1914), § 2.1.

Kersey v. Harbin, 531 S.W.2d 76 (Mo. Ct. of App. 1975), § 9.4.

Keyishian v. Board of Regents (N.Y.), 385 U.S. 589, 87 S. Ct. 675 (1967), § 5.3.

Kissick v. Garland Independent School District, 330 S.W.2d 708 (Ct. of Civ. App. of Texas 1959), § 3.8.

Kornblum v. Newark Unified School District, 37 Cal. App. 3d 623, 112 Cal. Rptr. 457 (1974), § 10.3.

Ladson v. Board of Education of Union Free School District No. 9, 323 N.Y.S.2d 545 (Sup. Ct. 1971), § 4.5.

Lee v. Mason County Board of Education, 490 F.2d 458 (5th Cir. 1974), § 4.4.

Leonard v. School Committee of Attleboro, 349 Mass. 704, 212 N.E.2d 468 (1965), § 3.1.

L'Hommedieu v. Board of Regents, 196 Misc. 686, 93 N.Y.S.2d 274 (1949), § 5.1.

Los Angeles Teachers Union v. Los Angeles City Board of Education, 78 Cal. Rptr. 723 (1969), § 7.3.

Lusk v. Estes, 361 F. Supp. 653 (U.S.D.C.N.D. Texas 1973), § 7.3.

Mailloux v. Kiley, 323 F. Supp. 1387 (Mass. 1971), § 10.2.

Maria R., In re, 366 N.Y.S.2d 309 (Family Court, City of N.Y. 1975), § 1.3.

McCollum v. Board of Education (Ill.), 333 U.S. 203, 68 S. Ct. 461 (1948), § 2.5.

McGrath v. Burkhard, 131 Cal. App. 2d 376, 280 P.2d 864 (1955), § 7.4.

McLeod v. State, 154 Miss. 468, 122 So. 737 (1929), § 1.4.

Medeiros v. Kiyosaki, 478 P.2d 314 (Hawaii 1970), § 2.2.

Metcalf v. State, 21 Tex. App. 174, 17 S.W. 142 (1886), § 4.3.

People v. Ekerold, 211 N.Y. 386, 105 N.E. 670 (1914), § 1.3.

People v. Scott D., 34 N.Y.2d 483 (1974), § 3.5.

Perry v. Grenada Municipal Separate School District, 300 F. Supp. 748 (Miss. 1969), § 1.5.

Pettit v. State Board of Education, 10 Cal. App. 3d 29, 109 Cal. Rptr. 665 (1973), § 6.2.

Pickering v. Board of Education (Ill.), 391 U.S. 563, 88 S. Ct. 1731 (1968), § 7.3.

Pierce v. Society of Sisters of Holy Names, 268 U.S. 510, 45 S. Ct. 571 (1925), § 1.2.

Pinellas County Classroom Teachers Association v. Board of Public Instruction, 214 So.2d 34 (Fla. 1968), § 8.1.

Plessy v. Ferguson, 163 U.S. 537 (1896), § 1.6.

Pugsley v. Sellmeyer, 158 Ark. 247, 250 S.W. 538 (1923), § 4.4.

"R. K." v. Board of Education of Township of Lakewood (Decision of the N.J. Commission of Education June 19, 1973), § 4.4.

Rice v. Commonwealth, 188 Va. 224, 49 S.E.2d 342 (1948), § 1.2.

Richards v. District School Board, 78 Ore. 621, 153 P. 482 (1915), § 10.3.

Roberts v. Way, 398 F. Supp. 856 (U.S.D.C.D. Vermont 1975), § 9.3.

Robinson v. Sacramento City Unified School District, 245 Cal. App. 2d 278, 53 Cal. Rptr. 781 (1966), § 3.7.

Rockwell v. Board of Education of Crestwood, 226 N.W.2d 596 (Ct. of App. of Mich. 1975), § 8.1.

Roy v. Continental Insurance Company, 313 So.2d 349 (La. App. 1975), § 4.3.

Rulison v. Post, 79 Ill. 567, 28 N.E. 68 (1876), § 1.1.

Salvers v. Burkhart, 339 N.E.2d 652 (Ohio 1975), § 9.4.

Saunders v. Reorganized School District No. 2 of Osage County, 520 S.W.2d 29 (Mo. 1975), § 6.3.

School Board District No. 18 v. Thompson, 24 Okla. 1, 103 P. 578 (1909), § 2.1.

Schuman v. Pickert, 277 Mich. 225, 269 N.W. 152 (1936), § 6.2.

Scoville v. Board of Education of Joliet Township High School District, 204 (Ill.) 286 F. Supp. 988 (1968), 425 F.2d 10 (1970), § 3.4.

Tinker v. Des Moines Independent School District (Ia.), 393 U.S. 503, 89 S. Ct. 733 (1969), §§ 3.2, 3.3, 3.4, 6.5.

Todd Coronway v. Landsdowne School District No. 785 (Ct. Com. Pl. of Delaware Co. Pa. 1951), § 7.4.

Tomerlin v. Dade County School Board, 318 So.2d 159 (Fla. Ct. App. 1975), § 6.2.

Valentine v. Independent School District of Casey, 191 Iowa 1100, 183 N.W. 434 (1921), § 4.5.

Vorchheimer v. School District of Philadelphia, 400 F. Supp. 326 (E.D. Pa. 1975), § 1.7.

Watts v. Seward School Board, 395 P.2d 372 (Alaska 1964), § 6.1.

Watts v. Seward School District, 421 P.2d 586 (Alaska 1966), § 6.1.

Weissman v. Board of Education of Jefferson County School District, 547 P.2d 1267 (Colo. 1976), § 6.2.

West Virginia State Board of Education v. Barnette, 319 U.S. 624, 63 S. Ct. 1178 (1943), § 2.3.

Wichita Public Schools Employees Union v. Smith, 194 Kan. 2, 397 P.2d 357 (1964), § 8.1.

Wisconsin v. Yoder, 406 U.S. 205, 92 S. Ct. 1526, 32 L.Ed.2d 15 (1972), § 1.2.

Wishart v. McDonald, 367 F. Supp. 530 (Mass. 1973), § 10.1.

Wood v. Strickland, 95 S. Ct. 992 (Ark. 1975), § 4.4.

Woodman v. Litchfield Community School District No. 12, 242 N.E.2d 780 (Ill. App. 1968), § 4.1.

Wright v. Board of Education of St. Louis, 295 Mo. 466, 246 S.W. 43 (Sup. Ct. 1922), § 3.7.

Wright v. Houston Independent School District, 486 F.2d 137 (U.S.C.A. Fifth Circuit 1973), § 2.2.

Zorach v. Clauson (N.Y.), 343 U.S. 306, 72 S. Ct. 679 (1952), § 2.5.

INDEX

A

ACADEMIC FREEDOM.
Teachers.
    Sex matters, § 10.2.

ACTIVITIES.
See Curricular Activities.

ASSAULT AND BATTERY.
Injuries to pupils.
    Liability of teacher, § 9.3.
        Conclusions, § 11.9.

ASSIGNMENTS.
Teachers refusing non-classroom assignments, § 7.4.

ASSOCIATION, RIGHT OF.
Teachers.
    See Teachers.

ATTENDANCE.
Alternatives to public school attendance, § 1.2.
Authority to compel.
    Conclusions, § 11.1.
    State versus parental authority, § 1.1.
Compulsory and prohibitory school attendance.
    Alternatives to public school attendance, § 1.2.
    Conclusions, § 11.1.
    Discrimination.
        Race as basis, § 1.6.
        Sex as basis, § 1.7.
    Married students.
        Status, § 1.4.
    Pregnant students, § 1.5.
    State versus parental authority.
        Development, § 1.1.
    Unwed pregnant students, § 1.5.
    Vaccination as condition for attendance, § 1.3.
Discrimination.
    Race as basis, § 1.6.
    Sex as basis, § 1.7.
Married students.
    Status, § 1.4.

323

JUDICIAL EXCERPTS

325

JUDICIAL EXCERPTS

MARRIED STUDENTS—Cont'd
Barring married students from non-classroom activities, § 3.8.
Unwed pregnant students.
Attendance status, § 1.5.

MARRIED TEACHERS.
Marital regulations over teachers, § 10.3.
Sexuality and the teacher.
See Sexuality and the Teacher.

MORALS.
Immorality.
See Immorality.
Sexuality and the teacher.
See Sexuality and the Teacher.

N

NEGLIGENCE.
Teachers.
Liability for pupil injuries, § 9.2.
Conclusions, § 11.9.

O

OATHS.
Regulations concerning loyalty display, § 2.3.
Conclusions, § 11.2.
Teachers.
Judicial repudiation of oath requirement, § 5.3.

P

PARENTS.
Authority.
State versus parental authority.
Compulsory school attendance, § 1.1.

PICKET, RIGHT TO.
Teachers, § 8.4.
Conclusions, § 11.8.

PLEDGE OF ALLEGIANCE.
Regulations concerning loyalty display, § 2.3.
Conclusions, § 11.2.

POLITICAL CAMPAIGNS.
Teachers engaging in campaigns, § 7.1.

PRESS.
Freedom of press.
See Freedom of Press.

JUDICIAL EXCERPTS

330

TEACHERS—Cont'd
Association, right of.
  Conclusions, § 11.5.
  Fifth amendment.
    Invoking, § 5.4.
  Oaths.
    Judicial repudiation of oath requirement, § 5.3.
  Subversive organizations.
    Early judicial vacillation regarding affiliation with certain organizations, § 5.1.
    Employment of advocates as teachers, § 5.2.
  Testifying against one's associates, § 5.5.
Claims.
  Unsuccessful claims for immunity, § 9.4.
Dismissal.
  Conclusions, § 11.6.
  Grooming violations as grounds, § 6.5.
  Immorality as ground, § 6.2.
  Incompetency as ground, § 6.3.
  Insubordination as grounds, § 6.4.
  Statutory provisions for teacher dismissal, § 6.1.
Expressing opinions on public issues, § 7.3.
Fifth amendment.
  Invoking, § 5.4.
Grooming.
  Violations.
    Grounds for teacher dismissal, § 6.5.
Holding public office, § 7.2.
Immorality.
  Grounds for teacher dismissal, § 6.2.
    Conclusions, § 11.6.
Immunity.
  Liability for pupil injuries.
    Conclusions, § 11.9.
    Non-immunity for teachers, § 9.1.
    Unsuccessful claims for immunity, § 9.4.
Incompetency.
  Grounds for teacher dismissal, § 6.3.
Injuries to pupils. See within this heading, "Liability for pupil injuries."
Insubordination.
  Grounds for teacher dismissal, § 6.4.
    Conclusions, § 11.6.
Liability for pupil injuries.
  Assault and battery as factor, § 9.3.
  Conclusions, § 11.9.

JUDICIAL EXCERPTS

TESTIMONY.
Teachers.
Testifying against one's associates, § 5.5.

U

UNWED PREGNANT STUDENTS.
Attendance status, § 1.5.

V

VACCINATIONS.
When required for school attendance, § 1.3.

334